IT Procureme
Handbook for SMEs

The British Computer Society

BCS is the leading professional body for the IT industry. With members in over 100 countries, the BCS is the professional and learned Society in the field of computers and information systems.

The BCS is responsible for setting standards for the IT profession. It is also leading the change in public perception and appreciation of the economic and social importance of professionally managed IT projects and programmes. In this capacity, the Society advises, informs and persuades industry and government on successful IT implementation.

IT is affecting every part of our lives and that is why the BCS is determined to promote IT as the profession of the 21st century.

Joining BCS

BCS qualifications, products and services are designed with your career plans in mind. We not only provide essential recognition through professional qualifications but also offer many other useful benefits to our members at every level.

BCS Membership demonstrates your commitment to professional development. It helps to set you apart from other IT practitioners and provides industry recognition of your skills and experience. Employers and customers increasingly require proof of professional qualifications and competence. Professional membership confirms your competence and integrity and sets an independent standard that people can trust. Professional Membership (MBCS) is the pathway to Chartered IT Professional (CITP) Status.

www.bcs.org/membership

Further Information

Further information about BCS can be obtained from: The British Computer Society, First Floor, Block D, North Star House, North Star Avenue, Swindon, SN2 1FA, UK.

Telephone: 0845 300 4417 (UK only) or + 44 (0)1793 417 424 (overseas)

Email: customerservice@hq.bcs.org.uk

Web: www.bcs.org

IT Procurement Handbook for SMEs

DAVID NICKSON

 BCS

The British Computer Society
Publishing and Information Products
First Floor, Block D
North Star House
North Star Avenue
Swindon
SN2 1FA
UK

www.bcs.org

ISBN 978-1-902505-98-5

British Cataloguing in Publication Data.
A CIP catalogue record for this book is available at the British Library.

Typeset by Lapiz Digital Services, Chennai, India.
Printed at Antony Rowe Ltd, Chippenham, Wiltshire.

For my mother, Mrs C. V. Nickson.

Contents

List of Figures and Tables

Author

David Nickson is a well-established freelance supplier of IT sales and procurement consultancy with a broad range of experience over many industries.

He currently works mainly on the sales side of procurement. Clients include IT and business process outsourcers, facilities and highways maintenance, and training organisations.

Experienced in both sides of procurement, with extensive bid management expertise, the author has worked for a wide variety of organisations of all sizes. He has also acted as an independent advisor to a major energy supplier for an IT outsourcing procurement.

David has direct experience of SME IT procurement at the small end of the scale. His own and his wife's training business operates a small network including laptop and fixed location computers with a broadband WAN connection.

Foreword

Anyone can buy it: IT that is. This is definitely a fact: anyone can buy IT, but can anyone buy IT at the right quality, at the right time and at the right price? Probably not. The jargon alone is enough to put most people off. It was always considered that the jargon was created by the IT industry to keep the IT club elite, however, the speed of change can put most, but the dedicated, out of reach of full knowledge.

The basic procurement principles are the same; it is the consideration that is required for IT that is different.

During the early 1980s I was responsible for buying IT hardware and software for what was then a relatively large government organisation. There were far fewer supply options with large corporate suppliers, with heavyweight legal teams, dominating the market together with very few technical options. Most decisions were taken on purely technical grounds and price was much less of a consideration.

By the mid-1980s, however, the 'dumb terminals' running off of 'mainframes' were out and the personal computer started to take centre stage and 'clones' also started to appear. This was the beginning of 'low-cost' computers for the mass market, which naturally includes the small and medium enterprises (SMEs).

These days not only is the number of options available vast, but the breadth of the buyer's market is also huge. This has driven the supply market to push the boundaries on technical and price grounds. Buyers now range from large corporations to SMEs to the home user. A one-person business has as much right, and in fact need, as a large corporation.

This brings a requirement for you to understand your needs before you start to buy and to be able to evaluate the returns you get when you gather together the various technical and price options. Generally the large corporations and government organisations have the technical and commercial expertise to cope, although many still get it wrong. For the SME, IT procurement is likely to be a one-off or at best a very occasional purchase.

For relatively little money IT can transform any business but buying the wrong IT, which can include email, internet access, website building, word processing, accounting, stock control, ecommerce etc., can be crippling to an SME.

That is why SMEs need guidance in a no nonsense manner: this is just what David has achieved in this handbook aimed specifically at SMEs.

The handbook style allows you to concentrate on what you need to and will be all you need to guide you in making those business critical decisions.

If I were to leave you with a couple of thoughts it would be to concentrate on your business needs not your wants and to make sure that any IT system is there for you; you are not there for it (so do not be a hostage to the system). The final point was captured nicely by someone when speaking about a large enterprise software system who said 'it moulds like putty, but sets like concrete'.

Peter Ritson 2007

Acknowledgements

The author gratefully acknowledges the help of the following people in the preparation and completion of this book. Many others provided help on an anonymous basis and I thank them too. A list of organisations, books and other sources can be found at the end of the book; their contribution is also acknowledged.

Steve Breibart, Caroline Broad, Frank Dickens, Yvonne Dixey, Barbara Eastman, Tony Emmet, Matthew Flynn, Sue Mann, Michael Nickson, Peter Ritson, Suzy Siddons, Roger Wade-Walker, Michael Webster, Tim Williams.

Abbreviations

ATQ	Answer (ask) the question
ATTA	Average time to answer
BAFO	Best and final offer
BIOS	Basic input output system
CBT	Compute-based training
CD	Compact disc
CPU	Central processor unit
CRM	Customer resource management
CRT	Cathode ray tube
DPI	Dots per inch
DVD	Digital versatile disc
DVI	Digital visual interface
EPROM	Electronically programmable read only memory
FAST	Federation Against Software Theft
FTF	First time fixes
FUD	Fear, uncertainty and doubt
GB	Gigabyte
GHz	Gigahertz
HDD	Hard disk drive
ICT	Information and Communications Technology
IPR	Intellectual property rights
ISP	Internet service provider
ISPL	Information Services Procurement Library
ITIL	Information Technology Infrastructure Library
ITN	Invitation to negotiate
ITT	Invitation to tender

KB	Kilobyte
LAN	Local area network
MB	Megabyte
MHz	Megahertz
MTTF	Mean time to fix
OGC	Office of Government Commerce
OHSAS	Occupational Health and Safety
OS	Operating system
PB	Petabyte
PDA	Personal digital assistant
PDCA	Plan, do, check, act
PQQ	Pre-qualification questionnaire
PSU	Power supply unit
QA	Quality assurance
RAM	Random access memory
RFI	Request for information
RFQ	Request for quotation
ROM	Read only memory
SaaS	Software as a service
SLA	Service level agreement
SME	Small and medium enterprise
T&Cs	Terms and conditions
TB	Terabyte
TCO	Total cost of ownership
TSF	Time service factor
VDU	Visual display unit
VGA	Video graphics array
WAN	Wide area network
WEEE	Waste Electrical and Electronic Equipment Directive
WWW	World Wide Web

Introduction

When you start writing a book with 'IT Procurement for SMEs' as the title, you have a great fear that making it interesting is going to be a challenge. This was a needless fear; the problem was limiting the scope to make the task achievable and the book light enough to pick up. The real problem starts with the scope of the SME (small and medium enterprises) market.

> **DEFINITION**
>
> **SME.** An SME is an organisation with less than 250 staff. This is subdivided between 'small' with up to 50 staff and 'medium' with 51 to 250 staff. The 'small' category is sometimes further partitioned to include a 'micro' category with up to nine people. SMEs account for over 99% of UK companies (DTI Small Business Service 2006). Indeed 70% of all UK businesses are single person or small partnerships and a further 7.5% were 10 people or less, so nearly 80% come into the 'S' category. There were estimated to be only 8,000 businesses with 250 or more people out of 4.4 million UK businesses. An SME 'blog' site reported that the SME market turnover represented £1.15 trillion in 2004, although they estimated that there were only 3 million businesses. Whoever you believe, this is a large market and if they only spend a few per cent on IT, then that is still a lot of money and a lot of procurement activity.

So the scope of the SME covers everything from one-person part-timers up to organisations with multiple sites, possibly international, with turnovers into the tens and even hundreds of millions of pounds. Unsurprisingly the type of work that these organisations undertake also covers an enormous range. At one end of the spectrum you might have somebody making bespoke craft items in their spare room, at the other an international consultancy in the finance market. Your local garage is an SME, your doctor, your solicitor, your builder, plumber, newsagent, employment agency, toy shop, engineering firm, optician, scaffolding supplier, nursery, window cleaner, dentist, flying school, boat builder, 24-hour shop...; the list is practically endless.

You will find SMEs in almost every market sector and geographical region. The only real thing that they have in common is that they are not very large. This provides one of the first limitations on the scope of this book. It is not possible to cover all of the applications and industries that an SME might want to use IT for, and no attempt to do this has been made.

1

The emphasis is on how to go about procuring IT in general, rather than industry-specific issues.

WHO IS THIS BOOK FOR?

This book is aimed squarely at anyone in an SME who is in any way involved in buying IT. For the 'S' end of the market this will probably include anyone in the organisation, as they will almost certainly be directly affected by what is purchased. At the larger 'M' end of the spectrum there are likely to be more specialist roles such as IT, finance, sales and so forth. Even here it will still be relevant to a surprisingly large fraction of the workforce. So if you work for an SME then this book is for you.

KEY POINT

At the time of writing it was estimated (PCG 2007) that over 73% of UK limited companies had no employees: they are one- or two-person businesses. For this reason the book sets out to cover their needs.

WHY HAS IT BEEN WRITTEN?

Although SMEs might use IT for a wide range of applications, many of these businesses are still new to IT, even in the 21st century. In 2006 Lloyds TSB Business reported that 10% of SMEs did not use email and a third did not use the internet as an information source. At that time a fifth of those who used IT did not have a band connection. Stephen Pegge of Lloyds TSB Business said of the survey:

> Small firms have tended to limit their use technology to communicate and organise information, but have been slower to wake up to the opportunities these tools might present for purchasing, production and distribution. (Pegge 2006)

However, they are 'waking up' in increasing numbers, so SMEs are procuring IT at an ever-increasing rate.

Consequently there are a large number of SMEs out there who are looking for help with acquiring IT. This books sets out to help them.

HOW IT HAS BEEN WRITTEN?

To keep this book at a sensible length and to keep it focused and useable, the depth of coverage of some of the related subjects has been restricted. For example negotiation easily merits a book of its own. Where these restrictions have been applied references are supplied to further sources of information. It is always going to be balancing act between completeness and usability. No apology is made for erring on the side of the fast read: if you are reading this book because you want help with buying IT, then you are almost certainly short of time.

Much use has been made of mini case studies and quotes from non-specialists who have real-world experience of IT procurement within SMEs. This serves both to bring the book alive and to prove to the reader that, whatever problems they may be having, others have gone before and lived to tell the tale. This is both a 'can do' and a 'how to' hands on book.

> **KEY POINT**
>
> One of the biggest challenges in writing this book is the variation in size of SMEs. The communications and political issues found in a 250-person business simply do not apply to a freelance writer. However, they can learn about larger or smaller organisations that they deal with from the examples and descriptions presented. This may help them in future buying and selling opportunities with such dissimilar SMEs.

WHAT IT DOES NOT INCLUDE

Readers should be aware that this is not meant to be a book about IT solutions for SMEs. The case studies that are included are there to illustrate points relating to procurements only. Those looking for pointers towards good IT strategies are advised to look elsewhere. Even the IT-specific chapter is only intended to provide pointers towards things to check when looking at contracts, scope of supply and so forth; again those looking for a primer on IT should look elsewhere; a good starting point is the references and further reading list.

HOW TO USE THIS BOOK

The book is designed for use in two ways: you can read Chapters 1 to 6 and get an overall understanding of how to go about procuring IT equipment; or you can just read Chapter 1, 'The Procurement Lifecycle', then dip in and out of particular chapters as required depending on where you are in the procurement or which related skill areas are relevant to your needs.

Chapter summaries

1. The Procurement Lifecycle

This chapter provides an overview of the IT procurement lifecycle from first requirement through to maintenance, refresh and replacement or decommissioning. A major goal is to provide the reader with an awareness of what they may be taking on. This chapter can also serve as the starting point for the reader who wants to dip in and out as it summarises the complete procurement process.

2. Managing a Procurement

This chapter describes how to go about running procurements. We describe what sort of team structure, people and skills may be needed. Common problems are identified together with warning signs. We also explain how to act as an interface between the organisation and supplier and describe how and when to involve stakeholders and other interested parties, obtaining sign off and approval, and list other political issues to consider. The reader is provided with realistic views on how much effort is needed. We explain how to go about planning: what are the key issues and stages? The impact of a procurement on the organisation is also considered, for example, disruption, time needed to help specify needs, testing and so forth, together with mitigation strategies.

3. Needs and Business Cases

This chapter covers the first, vital, steps towards making sure you procure what you actually need. Getting a good deal on something that you do not need is not a good deal. It includes alternative approaches, for example for low-budget or one-person businesses and charities, and other special cases. The scope includes how to go about needs analysis, getting the right specialists involved, looking at options, internal sales skills and other related issues.

4. Risk and Procurement

For those new to IT procurement, getting a handle on the risks involved can be very helpful. This chapter looks at how to manage risk in a procurement, what to look out for and so forth. It also provides a brief introduction to risk management for background information. Specific examples of typical procurement risks and what to do about them are included.

5. Bid Documentation

This is another core chapter. A successful procurement needs to make sure that both the consumer and the supplier have a clear idea of what is required. At some point this will come down to documentation. This chapter looks at how to write the relevant documents, what is needed and how to organise matters. Examples and templates are provided that cover invitation to tender (ITT), pre-qualifiers, covering letters and feedback to suppliers (good versus bad) being precise. Thought is given to standard disclaimers, for example supplier meets bid costs, and the use of terms such as commercial in confidence, intellectual property and so forth.

6. Bid Evaluation

This chapter covers how to identify selection criteria (not just price), making evaluations and scoring models. A worked example using a spreadsheet is provided to give readers a starting point for their own template. We also cover how and what to report on evaluations, supporting decision makers and advisers. Financial concerns such as lifecycle versus upfront costs (e.g. effect of software licences, leasing versus purchase and so forth) and total cost of ownership are also considered.

7. Quality Assurance

This chapter discusses how to go about applying quality assurance (QA) principles to procurements and explains why you may have to fit in with corporate QA of either your suppliers or clients and what to do about it.

8. IT-specific Issues

This chapter covers specific issues that relate to the IT element of a procurement, although specifically not a primer for IT solutions; for example bulk hardware procurement, operating systems, desktop applications, software licence considerations, solutions, maintenance and support, helpdesks, IT processes and outsourcing options (although not those relating to 'offshoring').

9. Suppliers

The ins and outs of dealing with suppliers, issuing documents to them, supplier meetings and briefings, questions, reference site visits, giving them feedback and being seen to be fair, are covered in this chapter.

10. Negotiation

This is a skills chapter providing an introduction to negotiation skills with an emphasis on win–win strategies and maintaining long-term supplier relationships. This includes some practical exercises that can be used for self-learning and internal training.

11. Legal Issues

This is very much a key points chapter and guide to when to seek help rather than a detailed treatise. It includes what to consider when seeking professional help. It does not give specific legal advice, but does cover the main things to look out for. These include licences, intellectual property, due diligence and so on.

1 The Procurement Lifecycle

The book hangs off this chapter: we define a typical IT procurement lifecycle from first requirement through to maintenance, refresh and replacement or decommission.

INTRODUCTION

A good place to start when considering procuring anything is to look at its lifecycle. Product lifecycles have long been used in manufacturing to plan for their effective support and production and have proved effective. Taking a similar approach for an IT procurement provides a useful tool for determining what needs to be done to achieve the best results. A major benefit of considering the lifecycle of anything you are going to buy, not just IT, is that it gives you the information needed to make a better buying decision. Buying something because its capital cost is the lowest can turn out to be a poor choice if it turns out to have the highest running costs.

Much of the logic of this book depends on understanding this lifecycle so it is recommended that whatever else you read in this book, you read this chapter before dipping into any of the subsequent material. Also anyone looking for a quick start guide to IT procurement will find it here.

LIFECYCLE

Figure 1.1 shows the author's version of a procurement lifecycle; others exist, but they follow similar basic steps. Not all procurement methods are based on this concept: some consider that the procurement is complete once the goods or services are delivered. This may be neater, but it does not encourage a broader of view of the process.

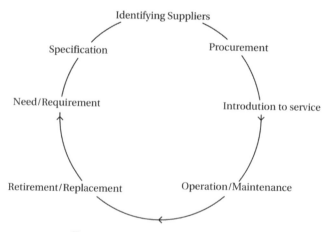

FIGURE 1.1 *Procurement lifecycle*

One may notice the similarity to the lifecycles that are found in many project management methods, for example PRINCE 2. This is not surprising as, when it comes down to it, buying something is a project. For that reason the author recommends that anyone struggling with a procurement takes a step back and applies basic project management skills and tools to the job in hand. If you can manage a project, you can run a procurement.

For those who look for formal methodologies it is worth noting that the Information Services Procurement Library (ISPL) includes IT services procurement concepts (see Op de Coul (2005) etc.). Although this is aimed at the larger end of the IT procurement spectrum, many of the principles will apply to the SME world and, where helpful, some further references are made to this. This methodology considers a procurement as complete once it passes into service: it does not view it as part of an ongoing product lifecycle, but does consider lifetime cost of ownership.

> **KEY POINT**
>
> Only when you consider this complete lifecycle can you come up with the total cost of ownership (TCO) for an IT (or any other) procurement. Consider the whole lifecycle, not just the obvious upfront costs, and do not forget to allow for training.

Needs and requirements (business)

Every procurement cycle starts with a need. This can simply be the marketing director wanting a new toy to play with; many a high-specification PC on a director's desk serves no function other than prestige. Usually it is driven by a real need to get something done: fulfil an order to a client, keep the accounts in order and so forth. During this phase the following points need to be taken into account:

- What do you want to do?
- Why do you want to do it?
- Where and when is it needed?
- What are the benefits of having it?
- What are the consequences of not having it?
- What can we afford?
- What is the cost justification for it?

There are various ways of going about this; anything from a chat at the coffee machine through to a formal needs analysis exercise using a formal methodology. The approach chosen should be consistent with the cost and risk involved. There is no need to spend all day in a committee when buying a new printer cartridge. On the other hand spending a significant fraction of your annual turnover on a new set of applications that the firm's future will depend on should be taken seriously. The bottom line is that you must ask, and answer the questions listed above before you do anything else. Chapter 3 provides a range of approaches that can be adopted to help determine needs and define the business requirements that come from them.

It is at this stage that the first pass at the business case is created for non-trivial procurements (not that you should buy anything unless you need it). This comes down to the following:

- Do you need it?
- Can you afford it?
- Is it mandatory (i.e. you cannot continue without it)?
- Would the money be better spent on something else?
- Would doing nothing be a valid option?

KEY POINT

You should not need to be technical to define your business require-ments; do not get bogged down in technology at this stage, and mistrust anyone who tells you that you should: they are probably after a fee.

Specification

The trick here is to specify what you want sufficiently well to be able to compare like with like and get what you actually want. Specifying in greater detail than required is a waste of effort and can restrict options that might be of benefit to you. However, the specification needs to be unambiguous and precise enough to enable a supplier to respond. For the non-IT-specialist this can seem like a real challenge. How do you specify what you want if you do not understand IT? The answer is that you should not need to understand IT to get what you require, but it helps. This is particularly true for SMEs that have little IT expertise in-house who are dealing with small specialist suppliers who have restricted business awareness.

Questions to ask at this stage include the following:

- Does the specification accurately reflect the business needs and requirements?
- Is the specification unambiguous?
- Is the specification complete with no yawning gaps?
- Is there enough detail for a supplier to quote against?
- Are the technical details correct (and do you have the expertise at hand to check)?
- Do you understand what you are asking for and why you want it?

Identifying suppliers

Before you buy anything you need to find out who can supply what you need. You also need to do some research about these potential suppliers to see whether you want to buy from them.

Some questions to consider for any potential supplier are as follows:

- Are they financially solvent: will they still be there when you need help in a few years time?
- Have they been in business for more than just a couple of years?
- Are they involved in litigation that might affect their viability or reputation?
- Do they have the expertise and support that you need to get things up and running?
- Are you able to assess this; if not, do you need professional help?
- Can the supplier help you further if you have problems?
- Can they supply you with verifiable references?
- Do you know anyone who has traded with them before? What do they say?

Procurement

This can be as simple as looking on the web or in a catalogue and placing an order. On the other hand it can mean conducting quite a complex procurement exercise involving requirement specifications, tender documents and assessment panels to inform the decision makers (admittedly this is likely to be true only for the larger end of the 'M' spectrum in SMEs).

The important thing is not to start until you have a good idea what you want to achieve (as before in specification). It is very easy to waste much effort and money, your own and the suppliers (who will not thank you for it), by starting a procurement before you are ready.

The essence now is to get the suppliers you have chosen to provide you with quotations that you can compare on a 'like with like' basis. To do this you will need to give the suppliers unambiguous instructions and information so that they are in no doubt as to what you want. The author speaks from extensive experience on the supplier's side where you can often see huge gaps and inconsistencies in the client's documentation but can be limited by tact when trying to help them put it right. Effort spent on getting it right will pay dividends and can actually significantly shorten the process because of a reduced need for clarification.

To support the author's case, the following appeared in the review of *The Bid Manager's Handbook* in *Supply Chain Management* in June 2003 is included, 'it is clear that bidders are more organised than their clients when it comes to procurements'. To be fair, the suppliers are bidding all of the time and have amassed considerable experience, whereas many buyers are relatively inexperienced, especially in SMEs when it comes to buying IT.

Some questions that need answering are as follows:

- Is the timetable you have chosen for completing the procurement realistic?
- Are the suppliers in agreement with this?
- Is the documentation sufficiently comprehensive for the suppliers to respond?
- Have you briefed the suppliers on what you want them to do?
- Is it unambiguous, as far as you can tell?
- Have you decided how you will choose?
- Have you established what your decision criteria are?

A significant component of procurement is evaluation: at some point you have to choose. There will usually be two elements of this, qualitative and quantitative, examples of which are given in Table 1.1.

TABLE 1.1   *Example qualitative and quantitative elements of an evaluation*

Qualitative	Quantitative
Track record	Price
Existing supplier (good or bad)	Lifecycle cost
References	Support cost, training costs and so on
Credibility	Performance (e.g. resolution, number of
Easy to deal with	users supported, disk capacity, central
Flexibility	processor unit (CPU) performance,
	memory capacity etc.)
	Delivery time or schedule
	Warranty
	Financial security and guarantees

A key point at this stage is to consider how you are financing the deal: are you paying upfront for the capital elements or are you looking at leasing options or business loans, or even putting it on a credit card (see *Finance for IT Decision Makers: A Practical Handbook for Buyers, Sellers and Managers* by Blackstaff (2006)).

Introduction to service

Once the hardware and software have been delivered then it will need to be brought into use. This will usually involve one or all of the following:

- **Installation**. This may simply be the physical process of unpacking it and plugging it in through to complex configuration and integration with existing IT services.
- **Testing and acceptance**. This can range from a simple 'did it work when we plugged it in?' to a formal demonstration and sign-off procedure.
- **Training**. Whatever it is that you buy, you need to be able to use it, and this can often mean training. There are many sad stories where companies have purchased excellent technology only to have it fail because nobody knows how to use it effectively.
- **Support**. Once you have it up and running you need to make sure that you can keep it that way, or have appropriate plans to deal with it being unavailable whilst being repaired or restored to service.

Some questions to ask at this point are listed below:

- Is there space (either physical or IT capacity) ready for it?
- Are any required support services in place?
- Do the people who need to use it have the relevant skills?
- Has any required training been completed?
- How will it be tested and accepted as being as ordered?
- What is the process for rejecting defective goods?
- Are there any actions required to validate any warranties?

Operation and maintenance

This is usually the longest phase in the lifecycle, although with IT this can be cut short by the pace of change. It can also be the phase where the highest costs are incurred. IT equipment itself gets ever cheaper, although software manufacturers do their best with new releases to try and keep you upgrading through higher performance requirements, but that is a different story (see Chapter 9). So, the upfront cost of new equipment can create a false impression of affordability. A classic example is the inkjet printer. These are almost given away these days, but over a relatively short period of time can use up many times their purchase price in replacement ink cartridges. Competing laser printers might be many times the price upfront, but their running costs can be lower (toner can be cheaper than ink).

From the point of view of the procurement project this can be seen as being the end of the formal process, even if it is considered to be part of the overall lifecycle. Thus, no specific questions are needed here: running IT systems is outside the remit of this book and is the subject of many books in its own right.

Retirement and replacement

Nothing lasts forever. Things wear out and the requirement for their use can disappear. With IT equipment there is the added problem that the pace of technological change is so fast that what was the right decision at some point can become the wrong one within a relatively short time. The simplest case is when the equipment is worn out: you either replace it with another of the same or review what you need from scratch.

There can be significant costs associated with the disposal of old IT equipment: it can often be classed as hazardous waste. Ideally this will have been thought of when buying it in the first place, but legislation can change and it is worth checking before trying to dump it at the local tip. Note that on 1 January 2007 the UK implemented the Waste Electrical and Electronic Equipment (WEEE) Directive. In short this means that suppliers have the responsibility for disposing or recycling old electronic equipment and this includes IT systems. See BSI (2007) for further details and Chapter 11 on legal issues for more information.

Questions to consider during retirement or replacement include the following:

- Is the equipment, software or service still required?
- Has the equipment, software or service delivered what was needed?
- Is it simply a matter of buying an exact replacement?
- Would there be any benefit in adopting a different approach?
- Has the requirement changed since it was brought into service?
- Is better or cheaper technology now available?
- Do you need to restart the complete procurement process?

KEY POINT

When you retire or replace equipment or software it is a chance, and a reminder, to review what you actually need for the future. Just because you have done things this way for the last few years does not mean you should just carry on in the same way. What has changed?

LIFECYCLE CASE STUDIES

The following two case studies are intended to illustrate the lifecycle in real life for small to medium IT procurements. They are based on actual examples, although they have been simplified for reasons of brevity and clarity, and the narrative concentrates on the highlights to illustrate points in the cycle.

Lifecycle for a hardware item

This could be a printer, a standalone PC, a copying machine or similar item that is there to do a job and has a significant impact on any IT that already exists.

Need or requirement

A small craft and jewellery firm that shipped no more than a dozen items per day (average) included an A4 flyer with their returns policy for faulty or exchange goods and basic terms and conditions (T&Cs). They decided that there was an opportunity to print a mini brochure or advertisement for their range of goods on the back of this. They wanted to do this in colour. They already had a monotone laser printer that they used to print batches of the existing flyer. So they wanted a new printer that could print a colour image, to near photographic quality, on the back of the existing flyer. It must be able to cope with the Christmas peak and be in place by October (when the Christmas orders first started to come in). It was then July. They had answered the basic questions of this phase, although they had not actually done this on purpose. The business case was simple: there was a reasonable expectation that extra sales would outstrip the cost of the printer within a few months. In addition ongoing increased sales needed to be greater than the costs of additional consumables: a modest goal.

Specification

The firm consisted of the proprietors (a married couple who designed and engineered the basic items) and a couple of casual skilled workers. They got together at coffee time and came up with the following specification. It would need to be able to print at least 300 copies per month and deal with a Christmas peak of up to 1,000 pages in a couple of weeks. It should be cheap to buy, easy to use and compatible with their existing equipment, a single PC running MS Windows XP. It should also be cheap to run. It needed to be able to reproduce reasonable quality colour photographs (not exactly a quantitative specification, but they would know it when they saw the results).

Identifying suppliers

This was relatively easy. The owners were sufficiently knowledgeable about IT, having been long-time users of PCs, that they knew the major manufacturers by name and were aware of various retailers, both online and in-store, that stocked them. Some initial research on the web and a browse through a computer magazine helped them gain an idea of potential local and internet-based suppliers. As this is very much a commodity item it was easy to identify reputable dealers, manufacturers and suppliers.

Procurement

The difficulty here could have been choosing an item, which could have been a long drawn out affair. However, a pragmatic decision was taken to look at just three or four models in a local store, compare examples of their print out, then obtain prices for the printers and their consumables. There was little difference in pricing, as is expected with such an item, but support options varied considerably in terms of onsite repair versus return to base and so forth. Although a sheet of paper and a pencil would have been sufficient to make the comparison, the owners in fact set up a simple spreadsheet (see the example in Figure 6.1, Chapter 6). They chose manufacturer A, but decided to pay a little extra to purchase it from a local supplier in case they needed support: the local company was close enough to drop the device in for checking if needed and had already provided this service in the past.

Introducion to service

This was easy, for once plug and play went well: it was simply a matter of unpacking it, plugging it in and connecting it up to the PC with the cable supplied. The only training required was to find out how to load it with paper and to change the inkjet cartridges once they ran low. The company's 'IT expert' spent half an hour figuring it out then got everyone round for a demonstration, that way she was not going to be stuck with this job every time the warning light came on. She also showed people where the instruction manual was kept and put a sticker on the printer with a link to the relevant part of the manufacturer's website where there was a handy fault-finding and frequently asked questions page. This was sufficient for this business.

Operation and maintenance

This amounted to keeping a stock of inkjet cartridges, one for each colour and one black so that there is always a spare. As soon as one is changed (and returned for recycling) another is ordered. As the print head is part of the cartridge a major component is being replaced each time, hence the general reliability of these devices and, hence, also the relatively high cost per page identified during procurement.

Retirement or replacement

So far so good, the printer is working very nicely and a number of new sales have been made as a result of the flyer. The small associated costs have been repaid many times over. However, the black and white laser printer is near the end of its life and a replacement for that is being considered. In the four years since that was purchased the cost of colour lasers, with their lower per page costs compared to the inkjet unit makes cost justification for this device questionable. It has only been in service for just over a year, but is it worth keeping? The capital cost is so low that it maybe worth keeping as a spare in case of breakdowns, but on the other hand space is at a premium. The cycle begins again.

Lifecycle for an upgrade from standalone to network

This is moving up the complexity scale for an SME. It is a more significant undertaking and this case study seeks to give an idea of what might be involved. Of course a bespoke solution might be trivial, for example just wanting PC equipment in a particular colour scheme for branding considerations. However, the example chosen here required knowledge and experience that the SME did not have. Such a bespoke Information and Communications Technology (ICT) solution needs a combination of IT hardware, software, applications, communications, security and training requirements: something non-trivial.

Need or requirement

Company B supplied plumbing and electrical items to local builders and trade professionals. Originally an entirely manual and paper-based business, over the years various bits of IT had crept in. The most useful was a standalone PC-based stock control system. This had been produced in the early 1990s by the son of one of the owners, a non-IT-professional but who was undergoing an IT degree at the time. It was effectively a holiday job. It was written in an MS Windows version of dBASE IV, a popular PC database system.

This was all fine when only one person needed to access the system, update it or generally maintain it at any given time. It may have been basic but it had done the job for over 10 years, the only upgrade being to move it from one PC to another. However, Company B's business had grown to the extent that one point of access to the stock system was no longer enough; it also wanted to have a second set of premises in a neighbouring town. There was also the possibility of offering an internet-based service in the future; the son was now working for the company and was keen to bring more IT into the business. The need for something new with a multi-site capability had established itself.

Specification

The owners held a number of meetings, also including the IT graduate son, the warehouse manager, the office administrator and a couple of the sales assistants. The first meeting was effectively just a kick off meeting where they agreed that the need was real and decided what they needed to specify before they could ask anyone to tender. They also discussed how they would go about the procurement, who would be responsible for what and so on, as this was not something they did often.

The outcome of this first meeting was a simple plan that established that the son would produce the technical documentation. The warehouse manager and office administrator would establish what the system needed to do in order to fit in with the way the business operated.

At subsequent meetings (there were a further four over the next few weeks), the documents were reviewed until they had something they thought a supplier could respond to. As part of this they realised that they knew enough to start things off, but they would need help either from the supplier or from an external source to develop their requirements over time. This was not something they could implement as a one-off: they had identified a need for ongoing support and development. Whoever they chose, either an external specialist or someone from the supplier, would be a de facto part of their business. This was going to be an important decision.

Identifying suppliers

As mentioned before, a spin-off from the specification exercise was that whoever was going to deliver this technology had to be willing to work closely with Company B and to be on hand to provide flexible support during the early days of use. They were looking for a partnership relationship not just a turnkey supplier. The local chamber of commerce was consulted, but turned up no members who could help. However, it did turn up a couple of leads from people who had used various firms for similar sized projects. Although the job was large for Company B, it was thought that it would be too small to get priority attention from any of the big name national IT companies. Supply of the equipment was not an issue: any of the reputable PC suppliers would do and their prices were comparable. The issue was the implementation and configuration side of the network and the applications: not rocket science by IT standards but outside the company's IT comfort zone. The same team who produced the requirements got together and decided to approach the two local suppliers already identified plus three others they had found via the internet. All of these were companies that had been in business for a few years and were relatively local, within 30 miles. As these were all organisations that were new to Company B, much thought was given to how to determine which to choose and what criteria to use. It was clear that the working relationship might be even more important than price.

Procurement

The requirement for suppliers to be relatively local and not too dissimilar in size to Company B meant that there were only four suitable candidates to choose from. Two of these had some kind of word of mouth recommendation, but none were really a known safe bet.

The plan was simple; there were only three steps.

Step 1. The first step was to issue each supplier with a brief overview of what was needed and a timetable together with a financial and reference questionnaire. Based on this two of the four were eliminated: one did not reply at all, so was not a good bet for a working relationship; one could not supply banking references making them financially suspect.

Step 2. Although not comfortable with only having two potential suppliers left, they decided to continue. Each supplier was issued with the detailed technical and user and operational requirements and invited to their own question and answer session. This was seen as important as it would give a good idea of what they might be like to work with. Both sessions went well and Company B learnt quite a bit from each of them. However, they got on with one supplier rather better, the relationship seemed to work better somehow, qualitatively they seemed to be more sympathetic to Company B's business goals and to understand the industry that bit more.

Step 3. The third step was to ask for a formal quote from each supplier. The quotes were similar but fortunately the quote from the favoured supplier, although slightly higher, was also the one that inspired most confidence. The response showed they really understood what Company B wanted to do, how their business worked and what it might need in the future. An order was placed and the losing company briefed to the effect that it had been close, why they had not be chosen this time and reassured that they might be considered in the future.

Company B had been lucky, many procurements go much less smoothly: you may end up with nobody you want to trade with and have to start again.

Introduction to service

The biggest elements of this related to training and installation. In particular the new system was 'client–server' based which meant a new way of working and the creation of a more formal approach to running IT systems involving networks and disaster recovery techniques. From the perspective of the procurement only, the fact that this went well with only minor hiccups, which were sorted out reasonably promptly, meant a tick in the box for long-term working.

Operation and maintenance

So far the system is performing well, there have been no major problems and the minor problems were either solved in-house or under the support contract or warranty provided by the supplier. No additional procurement issues have been generated from this and the cost of ownership is as expected.

Retirement or replacement

At the time of writing this had not happened yet, although should Company B decide to implement a web-based service then replacement, or at least modification and integration with new technology and applications, will be required. They have also identified that there would be benefits in adopting a wireless-based network and are also considering possibly outsourcing the operation and maintenance of the server to their supplier so that they do not have to spend time making backups, considering disaster recovery plans and so forth, although this would have role and responsibility issues for the son.

SUMMARY

It is important to understand that procurement is much more that just buying something. To be effective you need to keep the whole cycle in mind when making any purchasing decision. In particular it is essential to look at the TCO rather than the upfront cost. It is also necessary to revisit buying decisions from time to time to see what has changed and to make sure the original decision is still valid. An SME cannot afford to have dead money tied up in equipment or software that is no longer the right choice. Buy and forget is not a safe option.

2 Managing a Procurement

This chapter covers the management of a procurement at a glance: how to go about running a procurement; what sort of team structure and people needed; common problems, warning signs, timetables and common activities; involving stakeholders and the like, sign off and approval, politics etc.; realistic views on how much effort is needed; planning and key issues; and the impact of a procurement on the organisation (e.g. disruption, time needed to help specify needs, testing and so on).

INTRODUCTION

Knowing about the lifecycle of a procurement arms the reader with a basic understanding of the general sequence of events. This is the first step towards planning a procurement. In this chapter this timetable will be expanded to provide the basics for producing a realistic and achievable process that can bring about a successful purchase. The team you will need to make it happen is also covered here. This chapter is really aimed at those buying something at the more complex or mission-critical end of the spectrum. However, there are useful lessons to be learnt that apply to any purchase.

KEY POINT

Do not underestimate the amount of work you will have to do if you are procuring anything that involves bespoke or configurable components. At the low end of the spectrum, such as buying a PC, your time can easily cost you more than the IT equipment you are buying.

WHO DO YOU NEED?

Before getting into a more detailed plan it is worth considering what skills (and hence people) you might need to deliver an effective IT procurement. This is going to vary considerably over the SME range; if it is a one-person business then you are it, if you are a 250-employee company then there is rather more scope for variation. Similarly the scope of the procurement will make a difference too. Rather than list people, list roles: if you can fulfil these in one person then that is fine; if you cannot then you need a larger team. Table 2.1 shows the roles you need to fulfil for a non-trivial IT procurement.

TABLE 2.1   *The roles required for a non-trivial IT procurement*

Role	Description
Procurement manager	Person in overall charge of the procurement and responsible for day-to-day running, project management and so forth; not necessarily the decision maker.
IT specialist	Sometimes called the IT architect; person (or persons) who have the knowledge needed to specify, and later evaluate, the technical aspects of the procurement. Likely to be involved in any acceptance process.
Finance	Responsible for funding and budget decisions relating to the procurement (this can include both the cost of the equipment or services and the procurement itself). Accounting function for payment terms, cash flow and related items.
User specialist or representatives	Someone who is there to make sure that what you buy will do the job that is needed, and is aware of training and user needs, human resource issues and so on. Likely to be involved in any acceptance process.
Administrator	Responsible for looking after all of the paperwork, correspondence, filing and so on. A key role, not to be underestimated in terms of importance or work required.
Legal	Person who will define and evaluate T&Cs, licences, intellectual property issues and so forth.
Suppliers	Not actually part of your team, but without them you have no procurement; they need to be included in your plans.

NOTE

For more complex procurements this team may be subdivided further into specialisations, for example you might have different IT specialists looking at infrastructure and applications. Similarly training requirements may involve different people to user requirements. However, unless your organisation is at the top of the SME size range large procurement teams are unlikely.

Figure 2.1 shows how these people might work together in a team.

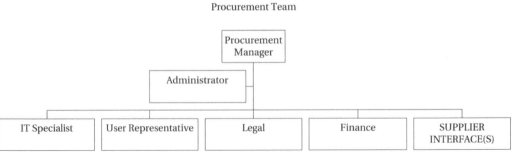

FIGURE 2.1   *Procurement team structure and roles*

WHY HAVE A PLAN?

For anything more than minor procurements you will benefit from having a plan. If you are just buying a new keyboard or something low cost where you are not too concerned about the detail then a plan is not really required. However, when you are dealing with something where either quantity or specification is non-trivial then a plan is a must. You need it to make sure that everything gets done, at the right time and based on the right information. Even quite a modest procurement will have enough activities to make ad hoc execution risky. Even a trip to the shops merits a shopping list: an example of a plan.

The benefits of having a plan are that you know:

- what has to be done, so that nothing is forgotten;
- who has to do it, knowing who to ask and avoiding confusion;
- when it needs to be done so that you can chase up if necessary;
- that the sequence makes sense and you are not trying to place an order before you know what you want;
- what to communicate to those involved so that they know what to do.

It all comes down to Rudyard Kipling's honest serving-men from *The Elephant's Child*. Most people just quote the first part, but it is worth reading the rest: people need enough time to get the job done with a reasonable work–life balance and the consequences of not having a plan are chaos with thousands of questions.

I keep six honest serving-men
(They taught me all I knew);
Their names are What and Why and When
And How and Where and Who.
I send them over land and sea,
I send them east and west;
But after they have worked for me,
I give them all a rest.

I let them rest from nine till five,
For I am busy then,
As well as breakfast, lunch, and tea,
For they are hungry men.
But different folk have different views;
 I know a person small-
She keeps ten million serving-men,
Who get no rest at all!

She sends 'em abroad on her own affairs,
From the second she opens her eyes-

(Continued)

21

(Continued)
One million Hows, two million Wheres,
And seven million Whys!

KEY POINT

If you do not have a plan then you can easily end up in chaos. Having a plan can only make life easier and increase the chances of you getting what you want, when you want it and at the right price. Remember that a plan can just be a list of things to do; it does not have to be complex unless the procurement is also complex.

WHAT TO INCLUDE IN A PROCUREMENT PLAN

Project planning in a nutshell is knowing what needs to be done, in what sequence, with what resources and dependencies. The starting point should always be the high-level activities and the timetable. This can then be broken down into more detail as needed together with refining the sequences and any specific links between activities.

As an unashamed advertisement for his own work, the author considers that *Managing Projects* (see Nickson and Siddons (1997); also listed in the BCS ISEB reading list) provides a suitable introduction to project management for the inexperienced. Other relevant titles are listed in the references and further reading; there is no shortage of choice in either methodologies or books on the subject. For the purposes of this book it is assumed that the reader has a basic grasp of project management or access to someone who has.

KEY POINT

Something that needs to be in any plan is a series of checkpoints (in formal methodologies these are often called gates) where you revisit the decision to continue with the procurement. Perhaps the need no longer exists or the costs look like being too high: just because you have started does not mean you have to continue.

Table 2.2 summarises the typical activities that might be associated with each phase of the lifecycle as described further in Chapter 1. Note that these activities relate to the procurement specifically rather than to more general operational/technical issues.

TABLE 2.2   *Typical activities associated with each phase of the lifecycle*

Lifecycle phase	Activities
Need or requirement	• Determine business requirements • Validate business case • Document requirements and business case • Top-level plan (if non-trivial procurement) • Risk management started
Specification	• Produce sufficiently detailed and accurate specification that meets the business requirements and needs of suppliers • Determine separate hardware, system software, applications software and network requirements etc. as needed • Determine QA requirements • Document the specification in sufficient detail to support the procurement • Revalidate business case if necessary and certainly check to see if it has changed since the previous phase • Update plan and add detail as needed
Identify suppliers	• List potential suppliers who provide the relevant products and services • Establish their size, capability and financial stability • Check that they wish to bid • If you have too many, consider a pre-qualifying process to make the numbers manageable • Check references for short-listed and winning suppliers • Brief them about your procurement plans and timetable
Procurement	• Manage the procurement exercise to choose the supplier that best meets your needs • Ensure sufficient resources are available to do the job • Use risk management techniques for both the procurement and the implementation of any service • Establish whether you are happy that you can work with them • Issue requirements and tender documents • Evaluate responses against your criteria • Score bids for comparison: this helps in 'like with like' evaluation • Evaluate TCO • Validate and compare prices (a major part of this) • Give feedback to losing suppliers as to why they lost (be polite and helpful, you may need them in the future)

(Continued)

TABLE 2.2 *(Continued)*

Lifecycle phase	Activities
Introduction to service	• Acceptance process and documentation • Training • Installation and commissioning • Final payments to supplier • Feedback to supplier on quality etc.
Operation and maintenance	• Document issues for consideration for future procurements
Retirement or replacement	• Review performance and requirements prior to determining whether the cycle needs to be restarted

SMART

A useful tool when running any sort of project, including a procurement project, is SMART. This is one of the more useful acronyms: Specific, Measurable, Achievable, Relevant, Timetable. There are other variants such as Simple, Measurable, Achievable, Realistic, Time, but they come down to variations on the theme. A short description of SMART is given in Table 2.3.

TABLE 2.3 *SMART elements*

SMART	Description
Specific	The goal and methods are clearly defined and the definition is agreed
Measurable	The objectives can be measured quantitatively
Achievable	Must be humanly possible and the project has to have all of the required resources
Relevant	The goal of the project or activity must be related to what the organisation wishes to achieve
Timetable	Defined and agreed deadlines

When planning any element of your procurement you should apply SMART to it. For example, you may decide to issue your requirements to the suppliers by 12:00 next Monday. It may be that the person needed to produce this is on holiday this week. Is it Specific (yes), Measurable (yes), Achievable (no: resource missing), Relevant (yes) and Timetable (yes). This is perhaps a trivial example, but it underlines the point.

HOW TO DOCUMENT IT

The guiding principle here is to keep it simple and short. The simplest plan consists of a checklist of tasks to be completed; a familiar example is the domestic shopping list. For an SME looking to buy a notebook computer, a printer and basic applications software, a simple list and trip to the local PC store backed up with some internet trawling should be more than enough.

For more complex plans where there are dependencies involved then the Gantt chart (first produced for military campaigns in 1903 by Henri Gantt 1861–1919) is both easy to use and understand. It also benefits from being supported by the majority of project management software packages. A simple example is shown in Figure 2.2, which shows how the logical links between activities and their time spans can be seen at a glance. This example is for part of a simple network procurement, but shows how this tool can help. In this case Microsoft Project™ was used, but there are a wide variety of commercial and shareware products available.

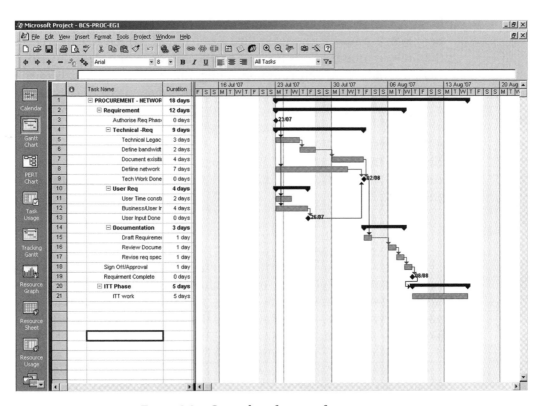

FIGURE 2.2 *Gantt chart for part of a procurement*

KEY POINT

When documenting a procurement save everything. You never know when something you thought was no longer needed crops up at an inconvenient moment.

WHAT TO COMMUNICATE

Having a plan is good, but it will only be really useful if it is communicated, at least in part, to those who are involved in delivering it. In fact a plan that is not communicated, and accepted by those involved, is useless. This also has to include those you are asking to respond: the suppliers. Although it is acceptable for you to specify the overall timetable you should make sure that it is realistic if you are going to get sensible and reliable responses.

Size matters

This is one of the areas where the diversity in SMEs becomes an issue. A one- to five-person company, even if it is procuring something complex, hopefully has few communications issues. If it does then it may not last long. A comparison can be drawn with the tightly knit crews of the Cold War V bombers, because they worked and trained together all of the time communications became so effective as to almost be invisible. Here the main focus on communicating a plan is on dealings with the outside world, the suppliers and any specialist advisers involved. The plan itself can be minimalist. At the other end of the spectrum where there may be multiple departments, internal politics, unclear lines of communication and responsibility etc. then you need to go for a comprehensive and clear plan that dots all of the 'i's and crosses all of the 't's. You also need to communicate the plan and make sure that those involved understand and accept it.

CHANGE

Change is always an issue with anything to do with IT. In part this is because of the pace of change of the technology. In 1965, Intel co-founder Gordon Moore described how he saw the future. His prediction, now popularly known as Moore's Law, states that the number of transistors on a chip doubles about every two years. The consequence of this has been the increasing price/performance ratio for IT. Over 40 years later this law is still holding. In fact the law seems to hold for everything, with the possible exception of software, in the IT industry. Five years ago a colour laser printer would have been a big ticket item for an SME; at the time of writing network-enabled colour laser printers were under £200 and dropping in price. So any procurement that takes more than a few months can mean that the original business case can have changed. Usually it just means that the hardware got cheaper, but this can mean that the original choice needs revalidating.

The other reason that change is an issue for IT procurement is complexity.

COMMON PROBLEMS

The top three are communication, timetable and resources. Change tends to impact all three of these, which is why it has been dealt with in its own section.

Communication

As with projects the main causes of problems in procurements tend to be communications or resource problems. This may show up in the shape of inadequate information, unclear requirements, poorly communicated information (internally or externally), misunderstood requirements by the supplier, undocumented assumptions, insufficient funds to complete the purchase and so forth.

> **CASE STUDY**
>
> The old chestnut, 'assume makes an ass of you and me' applies here. The real example we outline here was entirely a communication problem. The client wanted a new PC and placed an order with the supplier they had used in the past. They ordered the same model that they had ordered six months earlier. When it arrived the system had a different, newer version of the operating system (OS) than the previous machine. The supplier shipped the latest version by default; they assumed that this is what people needed (and indeed their website had the correct details on it, but the client just issued a repeat order without checking). The client assumed that by ordering the same item you would get the same thing. In fact if you wanted the older operating system you had to ask for it. The supplier wanted to make an extra charge for changing the OS, referring to their T&Cs; they could have been more accommodating, but you can see their point of view. The client made do with the newer software accepting that it took the user a few days to get up to speed with it.

Timetable

The next major source of problems is the timetable. Once you have decided that you want something, you tend to want it instantly. This will give any supplier problems and can become a continuing source of strife from the day you place an order to the day you start using the equipment. The only real solution to this is to have realistic plans that are accepted by both sides. As the buyer you can help this by asking the supplier whether they can really meet the timetable and making sure that you know what you need to do to facilitate this. However, where the new acquisition is related to revenue growth, or just maintaining money-generating business, any delay becomes a bone of contention.

KEY POINT

Time is usually related to cost. It can be useful to define your timetable in terms of what it costs you if you do not meet it. You can then validate your timetable accordingly knowing what you can afford to spend to meet it, or what you can save if you accept delay. Even cases where you have to make a change to meet regulatory requirements comes into this category: what does it cost you to cease trading while you complete the procurement?

Resources

Our third common cause of problems is resources. This is usually because there are not sufficient resources, either people or finance, although on occasion 'too many cooks' or 'how many people can dig the same hole at the same time' can be just as bad. They can combine: the expert you need may be too expensive for the budget you had in mind. Another factor can be when the resource is available. In a small company it can be difficult to free someone up to work on a procurement as they are needed full time to deliver their 'day job'.

KEY POINT

Do not underestimate the amount of work involved and its potential impact on a small organisation. Even a relatively simple exercise can tie up a significant part of an SME's capacity, potentially to the detriment of revenue-generating work. Plan for this and seek help as needed.

CASE STUDY

Person A was the only employee in the company (a small engineering business specialising in remote monitoring of mechanical equipment) with the technical knowledge needed to produce the technical specification that the suppliers needed in order to quote. In particular Person A was the only employee who knew enough about existing equipment to define the constraints on compatibility that the supplier had to meet. Unfortunately Person A was needed at a remote site to install the IT communications-related elements of a system for a major client. The simple answer was to get a contractor in to do an audit and produce a draft specification that could then be checked via email. In fact this is what was done, but it increased the cost of the procurement by over £1,000 representing 15% of the procurement budget. The other option was to delay until Person A was free. However, this had already been done twice and it was decided to bite the bullet rather than risking a series of indefinite delays.

WARNING SIGNS

Although it can come as surprise there are often warning signs that things are going wrong. Unsurprisingly they are related to the common causes referred to before. However, they are worth looking out for: these specific warning signs have been seen in the wider project management arena, but they are also very relevant to procurements. Table 2.4 shows some of them and suggests what you can do if they occur to remedy the situation before it gets out of hand. Even if you have a very small team, it is worth checking to see if any of these things are happening. Even one-person businesses can get carried away when on a buying spree and forget what they actually need.

TABLE **2.4** *Problems and warning signs*

Problem	Description and symptoms
Lack of understanding or misunderstanding	Spotting this is dependant on someone who is in a position to do something about it, knowing what should be done. A lack of understanding may mean that people will not do the right things; they will not know what they were meant to do. Misunderstanding means that they do something other than what was required. Either way this communication problem can have serious consequences. The root cause is a failure to check that effective communication is happening.
	The warning sign is that the wrong activities are being undertaken, or in the wrong sequence.
Actions consistently uncompleted	This is usually easy to spot. Things are simply not getting done. This may be because people do not have the time to do the work because they are too busy with their day job. It may be because they did not know they were supposed to be doing it (see previous entry); it may be because there is nobody with the right skills available to do the job.
Scope creep	This can happen even if you are just replacing a PC: you can end up adding in all sorts of options you do not need. For example, a procurement starts with well-defined boundaries, such as a new PC for keeping track of invoices and expenses using a spreadsheet. This can quickly spiral out of control: 'While we're at it why don't we look at using it to reconcile bank statements and analyse cash flow? Better ask our accountants what they think'; they suggest using a package that they use themselves, 'It will help with the audit...' and so it goes on. This is related to another warning sign, uncontrolled change. The warning sign is that the procurement is slowly growing without actually making any progress towards completion. The value of what is required increases with time.

(Continued)

TABLE 2.4 *(Continued)*

Problem	Description and symptoms
Uncontrolled change	The problem is that every time someone thinks of part of the procurement that they want changed it is done without question. For example, they might remember that they want the stock control system to record colour as well as weight and quantity. A few days later they decide they need pattern as well. Each time they mention this to the person producing the requirement, they just rewrite the specification. It either never gets finished or the supplier is forever receiving updates. The warning sign is similar to that of scope creep, but at a lower level. The scope of the procurement remains similar, but the actual specification of what you want never stabilises. The size of the overall procurement does not change, but there is never a stable definition of what you want to buy.
Gaps in plan	Not always easy to spot unless you have a good understanding of what needs to be done. The giveaway is where there are obvious missing links in the chain. For example, nobody has been allocated to produce a requirements document for the supplier or, more likely, nobody has been tasked with being available to answer the supplier's questions. Of course, there has to be a plan to see the gaps in; perhaps a more worrying sign is the lack of a plan.
Lack of staff or resources to do the job	At the 'S' end of the SME market, lack of resources tends to be very visible: there is nobody to do the work and you quickly see nothing is happening. Where the organisation is bigger, say with a dozen or more employees, then the chances of resource issues being missed increases. The giveaway is work being identified but nobody being responsible for doing it. Another slant on this concerns having resource (people) but not necessarily with the right skills. Make sure that the person responsible can actually do the work needed. The warning sign is that the work is not getting done and that nobody seems to be doing it.

SAMPLE PLAN FOR A SMALL TO MEDIUM PROCUREMENT

A non-trivial plan is provided here as an example or template. This is based on part of a real procurement exercise, structured within the framework given in Table 2.2. It would have been too lengthy to include the entire procurement and would not have added any useful additional information for the reader. There was also a simple risk to go with this; see Chapter 4 for guidelines on risk management in overview and specific areas of risk for procurements.

Figure 2.3 shows part of the Gantt chart for the early phases. It shows how the chart includes the resources needed. These are based on those given in the earlier organisation chart for a procurement team.

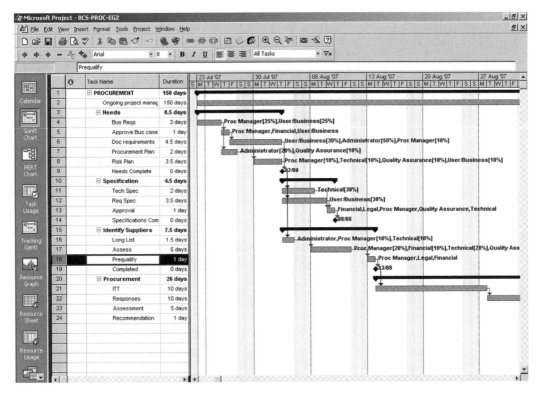

FIGURE 2.3   *Gantt chart for the early phases of a small to medium procurement*

For any plan you should ask the following questions:

- Do you have people to cover all of the roles needed to complete the procurement team?
- Do you have a plan that covers all critical activities and allocates owners and times to them?
- Have you communicated the plan to all those who need to know about it?
- Have you got their acceptance and understanding of what is in the plan?

THE MINIMUM

Even when you are buying something trivial you can benefit from a simple plan. After all, a shopping list is a plan: it says what you want and where to get it (and by implication when you want it: when you go to the shops).

A minimalist procurement plan, say for buying consumables, would include the following items:

- What do you want?
- How many do you want?

- How much can you afford to pay?
- How do you intend to pay?
- Will you collect or do you want them delivered?
- If so, where do you want them delivered?
- When do want them delivered?

Even this may sound like overkill, but an example given to me by one SME was that they walked down to the shops to buy paper, then realised that they could not carry 10 reams of paper back with them. They then had to make the trip again with a car.

SUMMARY

A procurement is a project, it needs the same processes and disciplines as any other project if you want a successful outcome. To keep you on the straight and narrow always check what you are doing against the SMART criteria: if any part of your plan fails this test then revisit it. Have one person who owns the overall procurement process with responsibility for keeping it on track. They need not be the decision maker, although it can help if they are. Make sure that everyone involved knows what is expected of them and when. Finally do not forget to make the suppliers part of your plans: they are the ones giving you the information you need, help them by being realistic in your timescales.

3 Needs and Business Cases

At a glance, this chapter covers making sure you procure what you actually need, alternative approaches (e.g. for low budgets, one-person businesses and charities), needs analysis, getting the right specialists involved, looking at options and internal sales skills.

INTRODUCTION

A good deal on something you do not need is a bad deal.

In the procurement lifecycle outlined in Chapter 1 the first step was, unsurprisingly, determining what it is you actually want to procure. This may seem obvious but research for this book showed that sometimes what people purchased turned out not be what they actually wanted at all, an expensive mistake. Spending time early on identifying what is needed is not an activity to be rushed.

For an SME with little IT expertise in-house, the technical part of the definition of what they want can be the hardest part of the procurement. Knowing when to get help and where to get it can save much wasted time and money. This chapter makes the case for analysing your needs early on and suggests some simple techniques to help you and to document the end result to help you move on to a more detailed specification. It goes on to look at how you can translate your needs into requirements documents for issue to suppliers. Documenting technical specifications are covered in more detail in Chapter 8.

COST OF GETTING IT WRONG

For any procurement the costs of getting it wrong increases with time. Spending a few extra hours when you first think you need a new computer application may be boring and feel like wasted effort – you know you need a new something or other. However, if you get to the point when what you want is delivered and does not do the job you thought you wanted done then you can be looking at serious expense and having to run much of your procurement again. Figure 3.1 shows how the cost of putting things right increases with time. In *Project Management Disasters: And How to Survive Them* (Nickson and Siddons 2006) this figure was used to show cost of change versus time for a software development project; it applies equally well to IT procurements.

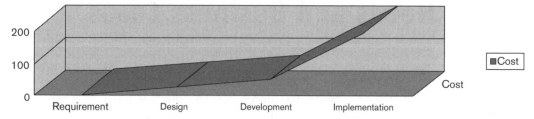

FIGURE 3.1   *The cost of putting things right versus time*

It costs many times more to make a change once something is nearly completed than it does at the beginning. At the identifying needs or requirements
stage the cost of making a change is relatively low as it is largely a paper exercise. The costs increase during the design stage (mainly because a change in
one item may require the reworking of other parts of the design, not just those
directly relating to the changed requirement). Once you get to the development and implementation stage costs ramp up dramatically. If you go to your
supplier on the day they are due to deliver your equipment or project it will
be expensive to have them take it away and deliver something else instead.

NEEDS ANALYSIS

> **KEY POINT**
>
> The amount of time and effort you put into needs analysis should be pro-
> portionate to the scale of the procurement. Buying a replacement mouse
> and keyboard require little thought; a new stock control system rather more.

Preliminary steps

Before anything happens somebody, somewhere has to say 'I want a
widget' or 'I need to fix this' or something to that effect. This can be anything from needing to replace a broken keyboard after coffee spillage
through to a stock control system or specialist computer controlled spark
erosion equipment. SMEs seem to cover everything you can think of in
every industry and market so the scope for IT procurement is endless. The
first step is to think of something and ask for it. The next is to find out if it
exists and how much it might cost and if it might be worth having.

Trivial cases

This covers low-volume purchase of consumables, low-value items that
are not strategic to the business and so forth. Typically toner and ink,
mouse and keyboard, minor one-off PC upgrades, new copies or licensing
of existing software for new users and similar items are included. In such
cases all that is required is to find out the price and availability from
existing and new suppliers and place an order.

That is not to say that you should not negotiate or look at alternative
purchasing options, but there is no need to go into needs analysis and

business cases to decide whether you need new toner. Chapter 10 covers strategies for negotiating a good deal.

Points to cover

Once the preliminary steps have occurred then the next thing is to look at needs in a little more detail. The areas the need to be covered at this early stage are covered in Table 3.1. Do not get drawn into technology at this stage and do not think about how IT might be used to solve the problem; just define what you need done.

TABLE 3.1   *Points to consider at the early stage of a procurement*

Area	Points to consider
Financial	Are you trying to reduce cost? Increase revenue? Both? Reduce the cost of meeting new requirements or legislation?
Customer related	Is it to provide a better service, needed to carry on, to improve customer resource management?
Logistics	Stock or material control, warehouse operations, goods in and out, delivery scheduling.
Administration and office	Staff rosters, who will need to be involved and use any system needed.
Security	What level of security do you need to: • meet your legal obligations; • protect your business's competitive edge; • look after your client's needs; • protect you from fraud?
Performance and capacity	Are there any specific performance needs, such as how quickly do you need it to perform a task? How many tasks per hour or day? Volume of work, frequency and so forth.
Availability	What hours do you need the service or system to be available?
Training	What training will your staff need? What is their existing skill level and what will they need to operate the service?
Processes	What existing business processes will be affected by the procurement? What may need to change and what are the implications of making the changes?
Growth	What growth does the system have to cope with? This may be in terms of increased amounts of information dealt with or with increased volume of transactions per hour. Should also include the expected lifetime of the system to help with defining any potential upgrade path required.

KEY POINT

Do not decide how the need will be fulfilled, just define what the need is: it may turn out that you do not need any new IT at all.

Brainstorming and ideas sessions

The value of taking time out to review what is actually happening in a project that is in a mess was a common theme when researching this book and seems well established. As shown in Table 3.2, one of the best ways to do this is to run a brainstorming meeting, as the freedom and flexibility of such meetings gives a good chance of hitting on a novel solution (or an obvious solution that people have been just too stressed to spot).

There are many variants on how a brainstorming session should be conducted, and several excellent and not so excellent books telling you how to run them. There are also training courses, although if you have time to go on one, then there is probably not a disaster in progress. However, because it is such a useful technique a brief overview or recipe is provided here for the benefit of the uninitiated.

TABLE 3.2   *A brief overview of a brainstorming session*

Step	Description
1 Initiation	Call the meeting: determine who can usefully contribute; we suggest that you have no fewer than 3 people and no more than 12 or things can get out of hand. If possible, get people outside of the immediate project team to provide the outside view. Only ask people who have relevant experience and skills; avoid senior managers who wish to be there solely because they are 'important'.
2 Location	Choose a venue, preferably away from the normal place of work, that can comfortably take the size of meeting and has a ready supply of tea and coffee plus plenty of white boards and flip charts with associated pens and the like. If you like, consider video-recording the whole process to make sure nothing is lost.
3 Set-up	Make sure that all of those present know what the meeting is for, where and when it is and what the topic is. Provide briefing notes on brainstorming if necessary. Set up the room and make sure any equipment works, there are flip-chart pens that work, blue tack for sticking charts to the wall and so forth. Check that there are enough chairs, and, once everyone arrives, get them settled down with mobile phones turned off.
4 Meeting	The meeting will typically have four stages: (i) **Briefing**: who is doing what, restriction on scope and areas of interest. (ii) **'Brainstorm'**: record thoughts and suggestions without any attempt at analysis or comment; anything from 15 minutes to an hour or so. Do not worry if people say the same thing twice, or similar things, just get everything written down without comment. The use of flip charts is recommended (white boards are difficult to take away afterwards), ideally with someone who can write neatly to capture the ideas.

(Continued)

TABLE 3.2 *(Continued)*

Step	Description
	(iii) **Analysis and discussion**: there are different ways of doing this; one is to group the ideas to give structure and remove duplicates and then quickly prioritise those that look most promising for discussion. The ideas are then discussed to determine whether they are helpful, what should be done next etc. It is important not to try and work out how you would implement any ideas in detail, as either the meeting will never end or the first ideas get debated well, but the later ideas are neglected. The discussions need to be recorded.
	(iv) **What next**: agree on who will do what to progress the remaining useful ideas. It may be that some ideas need further brainstorming. It is worth keeping the original flip charts and ideas for the time being as sometimes what was rejected initially may come in useful later on.
5 Follow-up	Hopefully, the meeting will have come up with some original, and maybe even project-saving, ideas. These will inevitably require some effort to put them in progress, and it is important to make sure that what happens next is documented and followed up.

Coming to an initial conclusion

Whatever method is adopted or path is taken there must be a point when a conclusion is reached. This will be either do something or do nothing. Either should be a conscious, not a default, decision. At this early stage you should only decide to do nothing if you are clear that there is no real need or it is obvious that it will not be worthwhile. If this is not the case then you should carry on until you have enough information to place an order or quit.

WHEN TO GET HELP

There are two reasons why you might need help when procuring IT, both relating to technical knowledge. The first is that you do not have enough knowledge to know what might or might not be possible with the available technology. The second is where you do not have enough knowledge to specify what you want sufficiently well for a technical supplier to understand what you need to buy. Keep in mind here that we are looking at a broad spectrum from buying a keyboard all the way through to bespoke applications. Somewhere along that spectrum there will be a point where you need help.

Only you can assess this; you may be an IT expert or you may think that you need a cat to keep the mouse under control. However, this should never stop you from identifying your high-level needs. It is the next step where you need an answer to the question: is this possible using available IT products?

> **NOTE**
>
> For those new to IT there can be a steep learning curve. The author interviewed one now retired owner of an SME whose scrap metal business used very high technology for reclamation but had little need for IT, other than as a typewriter replacement. When this person did decide to make additional use of IT, specifically for obtaining and tracking information on the commodity process, the technology was available off the shelf. However, it took considerable time to go from never having used a PC to being able to cope with the little glitches that are the day-to-day reality of a Windows™-based system using remote access to obtain data feeds for a software package with minimum support.

DOCUMENTING YOUR NEEDS

Once you have decided what your needs are it is important to document them. Although these will be higher level than a technical specification they still need to be captured. This will help you see if they have changed as you go through the procurement and get more information. What you thought you wanted at the start may not be what you find you need once you have more information about what else is possible.

In particular, they can be very useful for the suppliers as well as yourself; they may have experience of satisfying similar needs in other organisations and you can benefit from their broader experience.

Table 3.3 provides a structure for documenting needs that will cover most cases. Keep in mind that what you produce should be appropriate for the procurement in hand. Do not write for the sake of it.

TABLE 3.3   *An example structure for documenting needs*

Section	Content
1 Introduction	What your general need is, some background and stage setting.
2 Options	Choices for consideration, including doing nothing, that might meet specific and general needs.
3 Constraints	What are the 'boundary conditions' that apply to your needs? For example, any absolute constraints such as price, timetable, minimum performance, location, hours of service, growth, expected lifetime of service or product and so forth. These need to be documented clearly and unambiguously.
4 Conclusion and summary	Documenting the preferred choice and the business case that supports it.
5 Appendices	Any supporting material needed to support the above. Might include any business plans and constraints that apply.

NOTE

Organisations that operate formal methodologies such as PRINCE 2 will already have defined document structures and content that covers needs. However, that level of formality may not be appropriate for an SME, and even where such standards are in use they are not always appropriate for small-scale procurements.

NOTE

This quote, which implied significant technical requirements or needs in a non-technical company, indicates a common need in many small SMEs: 'Lots of legacy stuff kept going by our one techy! If it still works why change?'

Requirements specifications

This is the next step on from documenting needs. Hopefully the raw information was captured earlier on (see Table 3.1) and you are just tying matters down in sufficient detail to help a supplier understand exactly what you need.

Quality requirements should be captured at this stage too; Chapter 7 looks at QA for the procurement, but you need to decide what quality requirements you have of suppliers at this stage, at least in general terms.

CASE STUDY

This case study shows why specifying your non-technical requirements, rather than guessing a technical solution, is a better bet. Wainright's (not the real name) is a small retail business whose office printer had failed. It was an old laser printer and had served well for many years printing office correspondence, mail shots, invoices and goods received notes. The owner got into his car and went to the local branch of a retail computer chain. They thought colour printing might be nice, so they went into the shop and asked for a colour inkjet printer; they had heard they were cheap to buy and produced high-quality results. The store was happy to oblige and sold them one of reputable make. The device was connected up and worked as expected, for a few days. Then it ran out of ink. A new cartridge was obtained, although the printer was out of action for a couple of hours; this meant that some correspondence missed that day's post. The same thing happened a few days later, but by now they had decided to lay in a stock. A couple of weeks passed and the printer's paper feed failed. The owner took it back to the store and complained that they had been

(Continued)

(Continued)

sold a duff printer. Being a reputable company the store changed it for a new one, perhaps they should have asked questions, but they did not. The new device died six weeks later; the bookkeeper also noticed that they were spending a lot of money on ink cartridges, even allowing for what was now bulk buying. The owner took it back again; this time the store asked what they were doing with the printer. After the owner explained, the store said 'but that printer only has a duty cycle of 1,000 pages per month, you must be doing much more than that'. In fact the old laser printer, built in days when they were a high-ticket item, had been printing 20,000 pages per month; its duty cycle had been 48,000 pages per month.

Where did the owner go wrong? Instead of saying what the requirements were (a printer that could produce 20,000 pages per month and leaving the supplier to make recommendations), they asked for a colour inkjet printer. There was no way in which the assistant in the store could have known that what they had sold was unsuitable. A retail outlet is not going to have the time to interrogate everyone who comes in as to what they want to do with what they buy. Specify what you want to do with the device rather than specifying a technology or a model.

NOTE

It may be practical to combine documenting needs with the require-ments specification: if you can do this then save yourself time, do not produce any documentation you do not have to.

Technical specifications

Although technical issues are covered in more detail in Chapter 8 a brief overview is given here for those with requirements that need more tech-nical information to be included. Table 3.4 lists general technical areas with notes on what you might consider when identifying needs. Although some of these headings were covered in the earlier stages the key differ-ence here is that you are looking at technology rather than business needs: you may need external help here. You may not be able or wish to specify everything technically at this stage: do not tie a supplier down unless you are sure that you need to. This is a judgement call, for instance there may be technical constraints such as compatibility with a particular network technology or operating system that simply must be met. In many cases you should just specify volumes and performance targets rather than disk or CPU needs, although you may have some ideas of the minimum requirements.

KEY POINT

Keep in mind that if you do not have the knowledge to produce this in-house, you can always make it one of the responsibilities of the supplier to produce this. You are trying to solve a business problem, how it is done technically is not really your concern if you do not want it to be.

TABLE 3.4 *General technical areas and what to consider when identifying needs*

Area	Comments
Users	How many people need to use the system or service? Will they all need to use it at the same time? What constraints apply e.g. never need more than 4 simultaneous users out of a total of 10.
Processing performance	How fast a machine can process information. Usually the faster the better, but price accelerates once you get past a certain point (that changes with time, see Moore's Law).
Memory	How much space it has to work in: as with processing speed the larger the number the more work it can handle, up to a point.
Storage	Where your IT systems keep information in the longer term. You may need different technologies for different lengths and volumes of storage. You will need some longer-term means of 'backing up' this information if you want your business to be safe.
Connectivity	How you communicate data within your own organisation and the outside world. This will involve both internal and external networks. The speed and capacity of these networks will need to be appropriate for what you need to do with them. The faster they are or more data they can handle the more they will cost.
Operating systems	Specify any operating systems (e.g. Apple OS v10 or Microsoft Windows XP) that you are committed to or require the supplier to use.
Applications	These are what enable the IT equipment to do something useful for you. What applications do you need or have, what versions and so forth.
Training	If people do not know how to use your systems then you cannot benefit from them. You need to find out how much training you will need.
Support and maintenance	What is needed to keep things going after you have received it. Warranty is unlikely to be enough, unless you can afford to be without it for a day or so.
Availability	Specify working hours: the longest time you can accept the system to not work within a given time (e.g. must be available 97% of the time between 09:00 and 17:00, Monday to Friday, longest allowed downtime 2 hours, not more than once in any given year). This type of specification can have a significant effect on price. Related topics include disaster recovery and backup and restoration of data.

(Continued)

TABLE 3.4 *(Continued)*

Area	Comments
Security	Covering both physical and IT security. Keep in mind you can never have 100% security. However, you need to consider how important different levels of security are to you. For example personal information about your clients and access to your financial systems are likely to be more important than how many widgets in blue you have in stock.
Legacy systems	Technical details of any existing systems and applications that the new IT will have to work with, get information from, give information to etc.

KEY POINT

At this stage this is for your internal use; you can always change it later when you approach suppliers. You are not committing yourself to anything, just refining what you think you need.

The following quotations are all from organisations with less than 10 staff; they point out some common issues.

PCs are becoming consumable – why pay £80 per year for maintenance when you can buy new PC so cheaply?

Lucky to be ex IT or would have been in deep trouble. (Legacy systems support)

Make sure you try your backups out – not enough just to have them.

Financial requirements

For many SMEs financial considerations will have a significant impact on both technical and business requirements. It can often be the case that what you want will require imaginative funding and this is the stage when you need to tie down capital and ongoing financial considerations. Even if budgets are generous you need to establish financial needs before you can make any sound business case. To a certain extent unless you are looking at simple equipment-type procurements this may be a case of setting parameters: until you get the suppliers proposals you may not know even rough costs. Table 3.5 lists some financial areas to consider with notes on what may be involved.

TABLE 3.5   *Financial areas to consider and what may be involved*

Area	Comments
Revenue	Forecasts are always error prone, but you should have some basis for supporting increased revenue from a new IT system or service. A commercial website may provide a greater visibility of your services, but how much extra business will it bring in? It may not be simple to establish a reliable forecast, estimates always carry an element of uncertainty and circumstances change.
Capital costs	These are easier to identify than revenue forecasts. It should be possible to identify all of the upfront cost elements for hardware, software and labour needed to deliver your IT system and your supplier should be able to do this. However, where you are procuring a bespoke system then the IT industry's track record is not the best. Hopefully within the majority of SME procurements you will be on safer territory buying more or less off-the-shelf items together with some configuration. Do not forget your own capital costs, for example you may have to refurbish office accommodation, dispose of old equipment and so on.
Ongoing costs	These include: • funding costs such as interest payments on loans; • consumables such as toner, power, cooling and light, media, paper; • training for staff that are new to the equipment or service; • software upgrades; • renewable licences; • maintenance; • applications support.
Cash flow	For the purposes of this book cash flow boils down to the difference between when money comes in and when it goes out. When you pay for the IT services you procure makes a difference to its impact on the financial situation of your business. For example having a monthly account with a supplier that you then pay within 30 days can be better for your business than saving £10 on a PC in a retail outlet that you have to pay for upfront. This can also affect ongoing costs: a single monthly payment for all consumables may be cheaper to operate than paying half a dozen separate suppliers.
Cost of doing nothing	There may be implied costs that arise as a result of doing nothing. For example, it may be costing you money from late payments because you are not identifying overdue invoices. Similarly, you might be liable for fines because you are not keeping records required by new legislation. A new system might reduce your operating costs. Not having a commercial website may mean you lose orders to competitors and so on.
Alternative funding options	You do not have to buy all of your IT equipment and services brand new or at all (or borrow the money to do so) upfront. Alternatives include: • renting (you can now 'rent' application software online, known as software as a service (SaaS));

(Continued)

TABLE 3.5   *(Continued)*

Area	Comments
	• leasing;
	• outsourcing;
	• second-hand equipment (if you do not need the latest equipment);
	• returned 'new' goods from PC manufacturers (they often have specific 'bargain' outlets).

> **NOTE**
>
> Those who wish to find out more about the financial side of IT are referred to *Finance for IT Decision Makers: A Practical Handbook for Buyers, Sellers and Managers* by Blackstaff (2006). This BCS book goes into useful detail on all of the topics touched on above. It provides the reader with the skills they need to develop financial cases, understand different financing options and related issues.

BUSINESS CASE

Once you have a general idea of what you want, keeping in mind that this may change as you learn more, you need to make a decision as to whether it is worth having.

Table 3.6 provides the core topics that a business case needs to take into account.

TABLE 3.6   *Core topics of a business case*

Item	Description
Background	Summary (should be short) of key points so that the reader knows where the procurement fits in with the business.
Options	Do nothing.
	Proposed options (usually one to three).
	For each of these you need:
	(i) a description of what is involved;
	(ii) technical considerations;
	(iii) financial issues (upfront and recurrent costs);
	(iv) benefits (quantitative and qualitative);
	(v) assumptions and dependencies.
Evaluation	Financial, commercial and technical comparison of the options.
Recommendation	The option of choice together with the reasons for choosing it. This should include cash flow or any other critical measures and significant dates (e.g. break-even versus cost if it is a revenue generator).
Appendices	Any supporting material (perhaps brochures, references and so forth) needed.

KEY POINT

Always consider the TCO of anything you procure when considering the business case to justify it.

WHAT HAS CHANGED?

This is a question you should ask yourself every day. In particular when you are engaged in a procurement you can risk serious wasted effort and money if you do not identify a significant change that occurs between specifying what you want and placing the order. The business case that you have at the start will almost certainly need to be reviewed as the procurement progresses (see the key point on what to include in procurement plans in Chapter 2).

SUMMARY

It may seem obvious, but you need to know what you want before you can procure it. There are sufficient examples of this not being the case in organisations from the tiny to the multinational and governmental to make it clear that the obvious does not always get done. Take the time to think about what you want, get advice about what is possible with affordable technology if you do not have the knowledge yourself and make sure you document the end result.

KEY POINT

Getting things right early on will save you from a lot of headaches and wasted effort further down the line. It is worth taking your time over this stage however much of a hurry you think you are in.

4 Risk and Procurement

In this chapter we discuss how to manage risk in a procurement and what to look out for. We also give an introduction to risk management for background information and then provide examples of typical risks and what to do about them.

INTRODUCTION

For the more complex procurements (i.e. something that is either complex or vital to the success of the business) you will benefit from taking an informed approach to risk. This chapter is aimed at the non-trivial procurement.

Risk management and containment is a subject in its own right. A brief, potted overview of the subject is given here to provide a primer for those with little or no experience of the area. However, the purpose of this chapter is to give some worked examples, taken from real experiences, of the sorts of risks involved in a procurement and what can be done to contain or mitigate them. The reader can develop these examples to cover their own procurement and so improve the chances of a successful outcome.

> **KEY POINT**
>
> Although there may be no need to consider this for run-of-the-mill procurements, it is worth considering what can happen any time you buy anything that will be crucial for your business if it goes wrong.

RISK PLANNING: WHAT IS IN IT FOR YOU?

By identifying potential risks to your procurement in advance you put yourself in the position of someone who by being 'forewarned is fore-armed'. By being aware of the risks you will be able to identify warning signs and act quickly to minimise or eliminate their impact. In addition by identifying the high-risk areas it is possible to make a decision early on that the procurement is too risky to continue and therefore save yourself the pain of a wasted procurement. It is much cheaper to abandon things early on than to wait for a disaster after 90% or more of the effort and money has been spent.

The benefits of risk planning are an increased chance of getting what you want on time and on budget and a reduced chance of being ambushed by the unexpected. You also get increased peace of mind.

KEY POINT

Taking a realistic look at risk and being ready to implement appropriate contingency plans protects against potential nasty surprises later on.

Risk and contingency: definitions

Different people (and methods) have different definitions of what is a risk, what is a risk plan, what is a contingency and so forth. Unless you are creating a formal methodology it really does not matter as long as you and those you deal with know what you mean. Terms such as contingency plan, risk plan, risk mitigation plan and so on mean different things to different people. Here we are keeping it simple and hopefully clear by making up our own definitions for this book (they are in line with those in most methods, but the assumption is that you are not using them; if you are then you do not need this chapter).

DEFINITION

Risk. Something that might happen that will adversely impact your procurement (whether it is in your direct control or not).

DEFINITION

Risk plan. Documented set of actions you will take to reduce the chance of a risk happening, to reduce its impact (mitigation), and chances you knowingly accept (even if you cannot do anything about them).

DEFINITION

Contingency plan. Same as mitigation: what you will do if 'it' happens. You can also have contingency plans to deal with events that are not risks, but you get the idea.

It is now well established that risk management makes a difference and there are many books on the subject to prove this. Good risk management can make a real difference, but much of the time it is only paid lip service to. Quoting John McManus (senior research fellow in the Faculty of Business Management at Lincoln University and professor of management at the US Rushmore Institute) from an article in *Computer Weekly*:

> Most projects have a risks and issues register, but documenting an issue is not the same as doing something about it. How many risks and issues registers include factors that collectively should lead to the conclusion that the project is not viable? (McManus 2004)

This goes equally well for procurements, which are, after all, a specific subset of projects in general.

SOURCES OF RISK

In general project terms risk comes from events outside your direct control. Table 4.1 shows the sources and provides a brief description of what to expect.

TABLE 4.1   *Sources of risk*

Risk source	Notes
Political	For the small SME this is more likely to be an external source of risk. Local or national government rules and regulations, bylaws and so forth can all affect your procurement. In most cases these will not be things that happen suddenly, but they are things that should be checked.
	For the larger SMEs it is possible that internal politics may affect procurements; where different departments are competing for funding is a common example.
Technical	Essentially, will it work? If you do not have sufficient technical understanding or information about the requirement then you may find that you are not procuring what you actually need. In the worse case you may be getting something you cannot use. Technical issues may arise during the procurement that mean you need to change your specification for what you want.
People	Issues with people tend to be concerned with their availability or ability to do the work needed. In an SME there may only be one person who can perform a critical action: if they are off sick or called to deal with a client, then this can delay things. It is not just your own staff that need to be considered; those of the supplier or any subcontractor can be critical as well.
Commercial	The most obvious source of commercial risk is a lack of money, either at the SME or at the supplier. More subtle risks include T&Cs: the supplier may have the right to cancel giving a period of notice or may have the right to reschedule delivery. It may also be the case that the increased revenue forecast that was used to justify a procurement is overly optimistic. Such a risk is not one that you will be able to assess during the actual procurement.

(Continued)

TABLE 4.1 *(Continued)*

Risk source	Notes
Change	Up to a point all of the other categories can be said to come under this: if any of them change then that is a risk to the procurement. However, here we are talking about change as a source of risk in itself.
Process	Any business processes that you have, whether formally documented or not, can be a source of risk. In large organisations the sign off and approval, including technical approval, processes can be a problem. In an SME it is more likely that the supplier's processes are an issue. For example, they may be inflexible about payment T&Cs, delivery times and so forth.

In addition it is worth keeping in mind that risks can be either internal or external. You are likely to be able to do more about the internal risks than the external risks. For example, your landlord might decide to prevent you from using the car park for loading or unloading from lorries during normal working hours because it prevents patients from parking for the doctors' surgery next door. You have no control over this so might have to plan for delivery out of hours. It might be your company's policy to keep a car park space free for visitors and it is the only space left when the computers are delivered: you can change this. This is a trivial example, but it is worth keeping in mind that external events are harder to influence.

KEY POINT

Possibly the biggest risk for an SME is procuring the wrong product or service: if you end up with something that does not do what you need then both time and money have been wasted. SMEs have gone out of business as a result of buying IT they do not need or cannot use.

PROCUREMENT RISKS

There are some specific sources and types of risk that are particularly relevant to procurements. Table 4.2 lists typical risks, by source area, that are likely to effect an SME.

TABLE 4.2 *Typical risks for an SME IT procurement*

Risk source	Example
Political	(i) Government accounting legislation/tax regimes may change in the near future that may invalidate the system/reduce the benefits of having it.
	(ii) Environmental legislation may affect costs adversely.
Technical	(i) Incompatible with existing equipment.
	(ii) Insufficient performance or storage to cope with initial transaction or storage requirements.

(Continued)

TABLE 4.2 *(Continued)*

Risk source	Example
	(iii) Existing network not able to deal with additional traffic for new system.
	(iv) Difficulties in expanding network to all warehouse locations.
People	(i) Key personnel resign during procurement.
	(ii) Staff unavailable through sickness or customer priority etc.
	(iii) Third-party or subcontract specialists not available at short notice.
	(iv) Staff unhappy with introduction of new system.
	(v) Staff lack the skills to use it.
Commercial	(i) Reduced budget may make reduced specification or cancellation necessary.
	(ii) Supplier may go out of business.
	(iii) Cost overrun may damage your business.
Change	(i) Effect of change on current systems and procedures.
	(ii) New requirements or changes in requirements due to budgetary restrictions cause delay.
Process	(i) New processes required to realise full benefits of the system have errors.
	(ii) Reduction in level of service to clients while processes bed in.
Timetable	(i) The required timetable is not achievable .
	(ii) Supplier unable to deliver at weekends.

Table 4.2 is based on a procurement involving a combination of financial and administrative or operational significance such as an order processing and tracking system for customer deliveries.

IT-SPECIFIC RISKS

As well as the general procurement risks covered in the previous section IT has its own rocks to founder on. Table 4.3 covers many common risks and some that are less common. This is by no means a comprehensive list, there is not room, but it should get the reader thinking along the right lines. Use it as a starting point. You will need to make you own assessment as to the probability and impact for yourself (or employ someone with the relevant knowledge to advise you).

TABLE 4.3 *IT-specific risks*

IT risk area	Comments
Requirements	Poorly defined or incorrect requirements
Infrastructure	Physical space required
	Electrical power

(Continued)

TABLE 4.3   *(Continued)*

IT risk area	Comments
	Environment (e.g. heating and cooling)
	Communications (e.g. broadband, telephone lines etc.)
	Storage space for spares
	Security
Legacy	Existing IT equipment, operating systems, applications and so forth
	Existing investment in training
	Compatibility with existing operational processes
Support	Availability of spares (or lack thereof)
	Storage for spares and consumables (practicality)
	Technical support
	Training
Technology	The chosen technology for the solution does not work
	Availability of equipment or software
Technical resource	The supplier or yourself does not have the necessary technical expert resource available to deliver the solution
Management	Development processes
	Project management techniques
QA	Compatibility with established standards
	Technical documentation
	Acceptance procedures

SIMPLE RISK METHOD

There are various formal methods in the world that deal with risk, indeed there are as many risk methods as there are project management methods, possibly more. PRINCE2, the government's favourite project methodology, includes one of the more widely accepted methods. Most of the accepted qualifications for project management (e.g. those provided by the various professional bodies, see the organisations list at the end of the book) cover risk planning and control or management. It is now standard practice for any project to look at and plan for risk. The benefits are well worth the effort involved: a procurement is a project, so set aside time for it.

The risk method described here is a simplified version of those that are found in the formal methods. Doubtless risk experts will consider it somewhat light, however, it should serve perfectly well for most SME procurements and is aimed at those who have nothing in place already. Of course, if you have something in place already and are familiar with it then use it.

The process is based on a cycle of identification, analysis, planning and monitoring. Figure 4.1 shows the risk management cycle.

FIGURE 4.1   *The risk management cycle*

Identification

This is a research activity; you are looking for all of the things that might go wrong and negatively affect your procurement. The simplest way to do this is to ask everyone involved (that means you as well), including any specialist advisers, what they think may go wrong. At the same time ask them what effect it would have and how likely they think it is to happen. Do not worry if they provide sketchy information at this stage, the main thing is to collate risks, many will be duplicates. An example is given in Table 4.4.

TABLE 4.4   *Identifying risks*

Risk ID	Description and effect	Who	When
SP01	Installed application will be incompatible with some of the older existing workstations (no more than three)	AN01	01/04/08
SP02	Staff will be unfamiliar with the new version of the operating system to be rolled out with the application and so will be unable to use it	AN02	01/04/08
SP03	Data to be imported from the previous system may be incomplete	AN01	01/04/08

Analysis and assessment

Now that you have identified as many of the risks that you can in the time available (you can never guarantee to identify them all), you need to decide which risks require further thought and action. This need not be a complicated exercise or time-consuming. The first step is to rank them so that you can put in effort where it is most likely to be beneficial.

What you need to do is decide is how likely each one is to happen and how serious it will be if it does. You may have got some of this information when you asked for the risks to be identified. This can be done as simply as low, medium or high for each. Table 4.5 shows criteria for deciding what the level of impact will be. Probability is a straightforward matter of how likely it is to happen; Table 4.6 suggests percentages.

TABLE 4.5 *Criteria for deciding the impact level of risks*

Impact	Description and example
High	Very serious, something that will stop, seriously delay or significantly degrade the chances of success. Examples include: finance no longer available to proceed; essential equipment no longer in manufacture; building damaged by fire.
Medium	If this happens then it will certainly have consequences. It might mean that part or all of the procurement is delayed, although not to the extent that it threatens the viability of the whole venture. Examples include: late delivery of a workstation meaning that perhaps only two people can use the system on day one (as opposed to the three you wanted); the inability to print in colour for a few days whilst the correct printer is configured.
Low	An event that has little or no impact. Examples include: manuals available on disk only (requiring them to be viewed online or printed); part shipment with missing items delivered late but in time for successful project completion.

NOTE

Deciding the level of impact of an event is dependent on expertise. In the case of IT systems, knowing that a new version of an operating system will not support some vital piece of equipment you already use will require specialist knowledge and research. Some risks such as lack of space to put the new equipment are obvious, others are not. That should not stop you asking questions.

TABLE 4.6 *Suggested percentages for the probability of risks*

Probability	Description
High	Better than 50% chance of happening during the procurement process. This is something you think is quite likely. See the accompanying note.
Medium	More than 10% but less than 50% chance that you think it will happen: quite likely but a reasonable chance it will not.
Low	Less than 10% chance of happening during the life of procurement: something you do not really expect to happen.

NOTE

The percentages in Table 4.6 are arbitrary; this is a rough assessment not an exact figure.

Start with the table that you made listing the identified risks (e.g. Table 4.4) and use two columns to identify the impact and probability of each risk as in Table 4.7.

TABLE **4.7**   *Assigning impact levels and probabilities to identified risks*

Risk ID	Description and effect	Impact	Probability
SP01	Installed application will be incompatible with some of the older existing workstations (no more than three)	M	M
SP02	Staff will be unfamiliar with the new version of the operating system to be rolled out with the application and so will be unable to use it	H	M
SP03	Data to be imported from the previous system may be incomplete	M	L

Planning

There are a number of actions you can take for any identified risk, irrespective of its impact or probability. Table 4.8 shows common actions and provides comments on their use.

TABLE **4.8**   *Common actions that can be taken with identified risks*

Action	Comments
Do nothing	Ignore it and hope it never happens or will go away. This can be perfectly reasonable for something that will have either a very low impact or is very unlikely to happen. In other cases the 'Ostrich strategy' (burying your head in the sand) is dangerous.
Take pre-emptive action	Take action to reduce the probability of the risk occurring. For instance, if the risk is non-availability of a technical resource, for example your IT expert is on holiday or off sick, then you might arrange standby cover from a contract agency. Such actions are done in advance of the risk and may prove to be a waste of resource or funds if it does not occur. You need to balance this cost versus the impact of the event. See the first accompanying note.
Mitigate	Take action to reduce the impact of a risk if it were to occur. For example, should the system be delayed by a couple of days you might not be able to process customer orders thus causing them inconvenience. In mitigation you might offer them next-day delivery free of charge so that they receive their goods at the same time as they would have by normal post. You have reduced the impact of the risk on the end client, even if it is at increased cost or difficulty for yourself.
Plan a contingency	As the name implies, determine a set of actions that you will take should the risk occur. For example, the risk might be that the supplier of the network cables goes out of business; the contingency would be to place an order with another supplier and reschedule the installation and so forth. This may be non-trivial, the point being that you have a complete and worked out plan for what to do if the risk occurs. You would not expect to do this for low-impact or low-probability risks; even in other cases it will be a judgement call. See the second accompanying note.

NOTE

Much of risk management and planning comes down to judgement calls. You cannot afford to take pre-emptive action or mitigate for every risk. This is something that only gets easier with experience. You will, hopefully, have the experience of your own business; you may need to get independent advice about IT-specific risks.

NOTE

Contingency is a much-used word; consequently it is also a much-misused word. When making a financial plan for a project some organisations add in, say, 10% 'contingency'. This is wrong; what they are actually doing is throwing in some money for 'Events, Dear boy, Events!' (Harold Macmillan). We do not know what will go wrong but we know something will. Contingency, as the name implies, is something that you allow for based on (contingent on) a specific event happening.

Monitoring

It is not over until it is over. You need to revisit the risks from time to time throughout your procurement; things change with time. It is tempting to complete the exercise and the start of the procurement. Decide that you have appropriate mitigation and contingency plans in place, document it then put it on the shelf and see what happens.

Table 4.9 shows a possible update to the sample risks resulting in some being closed.

TABLE 4.9   *Possible update to the sample risks*

Risk ID	Description	Impact	Probability	Who	Date and status
SP01	Installed application will be incompatible with some of the older existing workstations (no more than three) **Update:** Two workstations replaced	M	M		dd/mm/yy Closed
SP02	Staff will be unfamiliar with the new version of the operating system to be rolled out with the application and so will be unable to use it **Update**: Ongoing, training in place, not delivered	H	M		dd/mm/yy Open

(Continued)

TABLE **4.9**   *(Continued)*

Risk ID	Description	Impact	Probability	Who	Date and status
SP03	Data to be imported from the previous system may be incomplete **Update**: All information copied OK	M	L		dd/mm/yy Closed

KEY POINT

Risk planning is not a one-off exercise: it needs to be revisited as the procurement progresses. New risks emerge, old ones expire, probabilities and impacts change. Ask what has changed at least once a week, preferably every day.

SAMPLE RISK PLAN

This is a made-up plan, based on part of a simplified version of a real procurement. The organisation in question did not use a risk plan and they were caught by surprise; they were lucky in that it was a medium-impact risk that they were able to work through. You might not be as lucky. The procurement was for a website with back office support.

Table 4.10 shows the result of the risk identification and analysis stages and Table 4.11 shows the actions taken for these risks and the resulting plan.

TABLE **4.10**   *Result of the risk identification and analysis stages of the sample risk plan*

Risk ID	Description	Impact	Probability	Who	Date and status
SP01	Installed application will be incompatible with some of the older existing workstations (no more than three)	M	M		dd/mm/yy
SP02	Staff will be unfamiliar with the new version of the operating system to be rolled out with the application and so will be unable to use it	H	M		
SP03	Data to be imported from the previous system may be incomplete	M	L		

TABLE 4.11   *Actions taken and the resulting plan for the sample risk plan*

Risk ID	Description	Action taken or mitigation
SP01	Installed application will be incompatible with some of the older existing workstations	Contingency budget allocated to replace the two workstations that this applies to if needed
SP02	Staff will be unfamiliar with the new version of the operating system to be rolled out with the application and so be unable to use it	Additional training available for staff with no previous exposure developed; delivered to those who need it in week prior to go live date
SP03	Data to be imported from previous system may be incomplete	Low probability, medium impact so no action taken

Another approach

An alternative approach is to assess risks at the activity level as well as overall. Here you identify risks for each element of the plan. Then you not only have a thorough understanding of what risks are involved but also when and where these risks occur over the life of the procurement.

> **NOTE**
>
> Different methods use different terminology for the lowest-level work units: some call them tasks, others activities, some work packages; they have in common that the lowest level is something done by one person on their own.

Table 4.12 shows a concept-level example of such an approach for a task or activity. It may only be worth going to this (or higher) level of risk planning for the largest-scale procurements that an SME is likely to encounter. You might have specific numbers and identifiers for individual tasks; these can then be used to track the related risks. You will find that using this approach can generate multiple versions of what is the same risk, for example poorly defined requirements might affect many individual tasks or activities.

TABLE 4.12   *Concept-level example for an activity*

Activity	Risks
Choose hardware supplier (CHS)	(i) Insufficient information available to make informed choice (ii) Suppliers not given sufficient clarity to respond (iii) Specification could lead to having to compare unlike quotes

The benefit of this is the level of detail; you are very unlikely to have any surprises if you follow this approach. It does, of course, assume that you have planned your procurement project down to the required level of detail in the first place. Perhaps there are organisations at the top end of the 'M' that might get value from this, but keeping in mind that over 70% of SMEs are one- or two-person companies no further information is given here. However, some of the books in the reference list will provide further reading if needed.

SUMMARY

For an SME risk management need not be an arduous task. You do not have to follow complex and overly formal methods to produce a risk plan sufficiently rigorous for your IT procurement needs. All that is needed is a simple list that covers the main sources of risk and what you are going to do to reduce the chances of them happening or deal with them if they do. As an SME is not huge, the baggage associated with communicating to a wider audience and conforming to standards is optional. Be pragmatic, but do not ignore risk: it exists whether you pay attention to it or not.

5 Bid Documentation

Here we describe how to write and organise bid documentation: pre-qualification, ITTs, requirements, good versus bad and being precise. We explain standard disclaimers, e.g. supplier meets bid costs, commercial in confidence and so on. We also cover correspondence with suppliers.

INTRODUCTION

Documentation often forms a large part of the workload for any IT procurement. Anything more complex than just restocking consumables such as paper and toner will need to be clearly and fully specified if a supplier is to be able to deliver what is needed. Furthermore, the documentation will form the basis for negotiations during the procurement and resolving any disputes that may arise later. It is vital to get this right. In this chapter all of the common elements are covered, although legal issues such as contract terms are left for Chapter 11.

To provide an added benefit to SMEs that might be in the market to bid for public-sector business, loosely similar terminology has been used to that found in the *Official Journal of the European Union* processes.

Specific documents include requirements documents, pre-qualification material such as request for information (RFI) and request for quotation (RFQ), ITT or invitation to negotiate (ITN), best and final offer (BAFO), T&Cs, correspondence and supplier presentation material.

The benefits and disadvantages of electronic distribution are also addressed in this chapter, as are instructions to bidders.

> **KEY POINT**
>
> Only include information that is directly relevant to the supplier. If they do not need it then leave it out: brevity is best.

GOOD ADVICE

At this point it is worth saying that you should not write anything you do not have to: it takes time and effort that can be spent on potentially more profitable activities. Before you produce any document (not just for a procurement) you should ask yourself these questions:

- What is this document for?
- Who will read it and what do I want them to get out of it?
- Do I have all of the information needed to write the document?
- Is it really needed?

Until you have done this, do not write a thing. Once you have done this and have a good reason to continue then do not hold back. See also the section in this chapter on writing style and skills.

REQUIREMENTS

Before you buy anything it is as well to know what it is you want to buy.

Case study

Overview

A small garage wanted to buy a system to do their basic accounts, support correspondence and handle invoices. They had a PC that was used to write and file letters but this was fairly old and nobody in the company really knew how to use it.

What they specified

They wrote up a shopping list of what they wanted: a new, up-to-date PC, with word processing, an accounting package suitable for home or small business use, a printer and something for connecting to the internet (some of their parts suppliers had websites and they thought it might be useful to be able to access them). They looked in some PC magazines and asked someone's technically minded 15 year old to help with this. The resulting, updated, list specified the version of software, the office suite, an accounting package, minimum disk and memory capacity, in fact a comprehensive technical specification. They did not know what it meant in detail, but it looked impressive.

What happened

The PC store happily provided them with a new PC, running the specified operating system with the up-to-date office software suite and off-the-shelf small business accounting package. It was shipped in well-packed boxes and arrived promptly three days later. The 15 year old unpacked it and installed all of the packages, because the garage employees would not have known where to start.

Outcome

The garage had sparkly new equipment and some manuals and a working system. Sadly, they had no real idea what to do with it. Their technical expert had done all he could, but his knowledge of accounting packages in action and business practices was somewhat limited. There was a distinct shortfall. This was very sad because it put the garage right off IT. They had spent what to them seemed a significant amount of money and had something they could not use. Perhaps if they had gone to the store with a list of business requirements without the technical detail the need for training might have been identified; even if it had not they could have gone back and said that they could not use it and ask what was the supplier going to do about it.

Lessons to be learnt

Specify what you actually want to do, what your requirements are; a technical specification of the equipment you need will not necessarily solve your problem.

KEY POINT

When you put together any document for a supplier to read and respond to, the easier you make it the better. For this reason it is recommended that you have as few **cross references** as possible within a document. Having to go back and forth is annoying; see if you can avoid it without being repetitive or long-winded.

The next three sections cover different elements of the requirements you may need to specify. They are provided in the order that the author thinks you should consider them: business requirements first, what you want to do; operational requirements second, how you need to use it; and technical requirements last, any constraints you need to apply.

Business requirements

What is it you want the technology to do for your business?

Table 5.1 gives a list of some points to consider under general business requirements.

TABLE 5.1   *List of points to consider under general business requirements*

Heading	Content and questions
Revenue generation	Is the reason for this procurement to implement something that will directly lead to an increase in revenue for your business? For example an ecommerce website, the ability to produce better mail shots and advertising material. Customer resource management (CRM) techniques can produce additional revenue and new sales leads.

(Continued)

TABLE 5.1   *(Continued)*

Heading	Content and questions
Cost reduction	The other side of the profitability coin. For example automating administrative processes, lower cost of producing printed materials such as brochures, electronic submission of documentation etc.
Regulatory	Changes in legislation or compliance rules can drive the need for administrative and IT systems. This may be for record keeping, audit trials or similar.
Quality of service	Use of IT to improve quality of service for clients through CRM, better record keeping, better information accuracy, improved speed of access to information and so forth. Improving the customer's experience of working with your organisation can provide a competitive edge and can increase repeat business.
Time to market	Ability to get information to clients more quickly supported by IT can help with time-to-market issues. For example you may be able to inform existing clients of relevant offers more rapidly by email than other means.
Market presence	Increasing the visibility of your organisation to the client base. IT can support this by producing better supporting literature, mail shots, internet-based advertising, commercial presence through websites and so on.
Business as usual	Is this a simple replacement for ageing or broken equipment or systems needed to continue doing business as usual? If so, are there any benefits to be realised by considering additional functions, taking advantage of new technology to improve value.
Growth	A common driver for new IT in successful businesses can be the need to cope with growth. It may be as simple as having to replace a manual process with an automated one because it is impractical or uneconomic to carry on using human resources.

KEY POINT

Your business requirements should be the driver for any use of technology.

Operational requirements

Here you need to specify how the technology will have to fit in with the way your business works.

Table 5.2 gives a list of points to consider under basic headings. Note that your specifications in this area do not need to be expressed in technical terms. Indeed it is in your interest to say what you want to achieve rather than second guess how or what technology should be used to deliver it.

TABLE 5.2 *List of points to consider under operational requirements*

Heading	Content and questions
Time constraints	Specify time restrictions for installation and introduction to service of what is being procured. Also specify the length of service expected prior to planned upgrades or replacement. Specify normal operating hours, for example this may be 08:00 to 18:00, Monday to Friday only for an office system, but may need to be 08:00 to 21:00, seven days a week for a garden centre in the summer. You also need to specify when the system is available for routine maintenance and software updates or patches and so on.
Physical requirements	Access to buildings, sites and maintenance spaces and any restrictions on the same.
Human resources	Human resource policies including equal opportunities, anti-discrimination and other legal requirements.
Business processes	Overview of existing business processes (and any new ones you wish the supplier to cover) that need to be supported.
Capacity	Volumes associated with the running of the service such as number and different types of transactions or operations to be processed each hour, day, week or year. For example how many stock updates per hour, how long information needs to be kept on the system for live or archived access and so forth.
Performance	This is related to capacity and reflects how much work you need the system or service to do. You need to specify how quickly you need any operation or transaction completed in order to provide the service you need. For example, how long to produce an invoice or a stock control report.
Availability	How much of the time do you need to be able to use the service or system? This is different to operational hours and needs to cover the amount of time you can afford it to be out of service, for example for repairs or servicing.

KEY POINT

Technology may well support new and better ways of working. However, you should not need to bend your business to suit the technology unless there is a very, very good reason.

Technical requirements

First thing to remember here is that you are not trying to design the solution for the supplier. Doing this can constrain them unnecessarily and if you are not an expert you might get it wrong. You are giving them the parameters they need to work within: the technical boundary conditions for their solution. If you are starting form scratch, you may not need this section at all.

Although a point was made of not having cross references earlier please see the section in Chapter 8 under 'Technology' where common IT terms, their use and meaning are described. This could fit in either chapter; on balance it was considered better to put it where it is. You will only need to look at it if you are unfamiliar with IT terminology when you are actually writing the document, you do not need it to understand this section.

Table 5.3 gives a list of points to consider under basic headings.

TABLE **5.3**   *List of points to consider under technical requirements*

Heading	Content and questions
Legacy	Specify any existing technical requirements the new application or equipment has to work with. For example what operating system, versions, current applications, email and internet connectivity, databases etc. Define which legacy systems must continue to work and be supported after the 'new' system or equipment is in place.
IT strategy	Technology platform that you have standardised on; you may have done this by default (e.g. you purchased an Apple computer because you work in a creative industry and everyone else has one, you have a 'Wintel' platform because you got a cheap PC etc.). In many cases this information will be strongly related to the legacy regime.
Physical and environmental	How much space is there? Limitations on electrical and telecommunications connections and cabling, air conditioning, access, stairs, floor loadings, access security, hours when building or office may be closed, parking and vehicular access and so forth.
Security	Specify any IT (and related physical) security processes you have in hand or would like to be developed. Consider firewalls, anti-virus, password format and update rules, user administration and so on.
Human resources	Define the skills level of any staff that will be involved in using the 'new' system if they may require training. Specify how many, when and where they will need to be trained.

KEY POINT

It may seem obvious, but if you do not have enough technical knowledge do not write a technical specification. If you start specifying technical requirements based on a poor understanding of technology then you may constrain your potential supplier into delivering either the wrong solution or a more costly one than you need. Remember it is the supplier that has to have the technical know-how; you just need to know what you want done.

PRE-QUALIFICATION

Most SMEs are very unlikely to need to go through any form of pre-qualification exercise. The term comes from the *Official Journal of the European Union* procurements for government business. Here there is a requirement to sieve out a long list of suitable suppliers from a potentially very long list of potential bidders. In the research for this book, the author was unable to find any example of an SME doing this. However, if you did find yourself swamped with responses to an advertisement for services, you might want to consider having an initial filter.

You want a short document that asks pertinent questions to allow you to make a top-level selection. Suggested areas include financial stability, track record for this type of work, references from existing clients, company size and expertise, availability of staff to deliver the work and a declaration of any impending legal action. There need only be a summary description of your requirements to allow them to indicate their willingness and ability to deliver. You would not be asking for pricing or firm commitments to bid at this stage. There are examples of UK Government pre-qualification questionnaire (PQQ) documents on the Office of Government Commerce (OGC) website (see the list of useful websites at the end of the book).

ITT OR ITN

This is the hub of the procurement documentation that you need; at a pinch you may get away with just an ITT and a contract.

NOTE

Terms such as ITT and ITN are frequently used loosely and interchangeably. They are similar and are frequently swapped even though they are different. An ITT asks the supplier to 'tender' for business; it implies a binding offer to deliver the goods and services required. An ITN asks the supplier to enter into negotiation for the supply (and by implication the definition of what is to be supplied) of goods and services. However, there is often sufficient wriggle room in terms of T&Cs, due diligence and so forth that an ITT is usually subject to further negotiation. The author's view is that ITN is a more honest title that reflects reality, whatever formal definitions might imply. Whatever you call it, as long as you make it clear to the supplier what the process is going to be then it does not really matter.

Table 5.4 gives a typical ITT or ITN document in summary.

TABLE 5.4   *Summary of a typical ITT or ITN document*

Section	Title	Description
1	Introduction	A brief overview of what you are doing and how the document is structured. It is worth including contact details here.
2	Instructions	What the supplier needs to do in order to respond, ask questions and so forth. This includes a timetable for the procurement and the format for the response. If you are asking for an electronic response (either as well as or instead of) then file format, your email address and any file size limitations need to be specified. You should describe any relevant processes, such as evaluation, due diligence and so on.
3	Background	Relevant supporting information such as why you are doing this, what it is for, context that will help them understand your thinking and needs.
4	Requirements	A clear description of both your business requirements and technical needs and constraints. Any timetable requirements for delivering the equipment or solution must also be clear. Specify location(s), environmental and site restrictions such as power, access and so forth. Other requirements to spell out include QA, operational needs (e.g. hours of service), security, staff training requirements etc. You may choose to split these into mandatory (must have) requirements and desirable (would be nice) requirements.
5	Specific questions	Questions to which you need clearly defined answers; these may be technical, operational, to do with project plans or anything you need a specific answer for.
6	Commercial and legal	Any commercial issues you want addressed; this may include questions about their financial status, any outstanding litigation and so forth.
7	Pricing	Define how you want them to present their pricing: you need to do this in such a way that you will be able to compare like with like. So if you want capital costs separate from maintenance and support costs say so. If you want leasing and hire options to be considered show how you want them too. Ideally present the supplier with a spreadsheet to complete. This then gives you the option of using these to feed directly into any evaluation model you use.
8	T&Cs	Present the T&Cs you wish to use, if you have them. If you do not then you must ask the suppliers to present their own.
9	Appendices	Any supporting material you think they need that is too detailed to go in the main body of the document. For example an inventory of existing equipment, building layouts, cabling diagrams, lists of existing software and version numbers, skills audits of staff who will use the system and so forth.

BAFO

Again, this terminology comes from the world of large-scale procurements. That said it is still relevant for an SME making a significant procurement where they want to make sure of the best deal or solution by having competing finalists. As you would expect this is a document issued to suppliers for them to put in their 'last' word on what they are offering and at what prices and T&Cs. The use of inverted commas is deliberate, as many suppliers can testify, because there can be further negotiation after this, but it is normally just between the buyer and one supplier.

CONTRACTUAL MATERIAL

Unless the SME happens to be a law firm or have its own legal department then this can be an area where outside help is needed. In reality you are more likely to need help in sorting out what the suppliers are offering than you are with your own T&Cs. In particular software licences are notoriously obfuscatory and difficult to understand.

CORRESPONDENCE

Inevitably there will be written communication with the suppliers throughout any procurement. This may be paper or electronically based. It should all be kept and easy to retrieve.

Answering questions

A significant subset of procurement correspondence, particularly in the early stages for complex IT solutions, will be in the form of questions that require a written response. There are two common ways of doing this: individually and collectively.

PRESENTATIONS (TO SUPPLIERS)

For the more complex procurement giving presentations and briefings or question and answer sessions can make life easier for all concerned. It can be very time-consuming to have lengthy correspondence with multiple suppliers who are all raising similar issues (see also 'Answering questions' above). However, documentation will be associated with these events, so this element is covered in summary in Table 5.5.

TABLE 5.5 *Summary of a presentation session*

Item	Description
Welcome	Who you are and who they are.
Logistics	Things such as fire exits, coffee and lunch arrangements and confirmation of the timetable.
Introduction	What the presentation is for and what it will cover.
Agenda	The schedule for the presentation with timings where possible.
Topics	The body of the presentation given in a logical order covering the material to be dealt with, for example background to procurement, procurement process, key requirements, QA and acceptance, how you will evaluate proposals and so on.
Questions	An opportunity for questions and answers; you may have some prepared for your client, they will certainly have some for you. Having a separate agenda item for this gives you the chance to keep the presentation on schedule and manage questions and answers effectively; have a chairperson to run this session.
Summary	A round up session where any actions are agreed, what next etc.

ELECTRONIC VERSUS PAPER

There are two elements to the electronic versus paper debate. The first is sustainability and green issues. The second is convenience and efficiency. Paper has the benefit of being universally acceptable, easy to look at and make notes on, it is simple to deal with, easily kept for backup or reference and harder to delete by mistake. It does lead to loss of trees and takes time to send or copy if that is a requirement. Electronic documentation is of itself 'greener' than paper and is trivial to copy and distribute by email and so on. It needs to be backed up and carefully preserved for future needs; it is also important to have master copies in case of later edits leading to confusion. Document management can be more complex for electronic material.

NOTE

Of course if yours is a start-up organisation or one with no existing technology you may only be able to cope with written material.

KEY POINT

The author's view is that for the complex end of the spectrum where there is significant tender documentation (e.g. for a bespoke solution) an all-electronic approach is best. However, when obtaining a written quote for off-the-shelf items, paper has the merit of being universally acceptable.

INSTRUCTIONS TO BIDDERS AND SUPPLIERS

Somewhere, and it must be easy to find, there must be instructions provided so that the suppliers know what it is they need to do to meet your needs. Instructions may be needed for any of the documents described in this section; rather than repeat this material with each part it is covered here. Some people prefer to provide these separately within a covering letter. However, it is more convenient for the suppler if they are all in one document; the less they have to keep track of the easier it is.

Table 5.6 lists what you need to tell the supplier. It is suggested that this information is provided very early on in the documentation. It is tempting to put it in an appendix because it is not directly relevant to the requirements and so forth. Best practice is to include it early: make life easy for the supplier and they are more likely to give you what you want.

TABLE 5.6   *Instructions for the supplier*

Item	Description
Timetable	Deadline for them to ask you questions.
	When you want them to reply by.
	When you will ask them for any clarifications or meetings (so that they know when you are likely to be in touch).
	When you will make a decision.
	When you want the contract or services to start or goods to be delivered.
Contact details	Who with and how you want them to get in touch. You may wish to give them an alternate in case of non-availability or separate contacts for commercial and technical questions.
Response format	It is helpful to specify what format and structure you want the response in. You may also wish to limit the length of response you wish to receive. This all helps you in comparing like with like and will restrict the amount of material you have to wade through. Focusing the suppliers on information directly relevant to you cuts down on marketing speak, waffle and brochure ware.
Commercial in confidence	You may wish to include information that is confidential to your organisation and might give advantage to a competitor. It is important that you identify this and make its disclosure an issue for legal action. By default it is recommended that you mark all your procurement-related documents 'commercial in confidence'.
Disclaimers	It is helpful to make it clear that you are giving out information that is only accurate 'to the best of your knowledge', i.e. that if it is wrong then you are not liable for wasted time or consequences (there are limits to this). A standard disclaimer is that 'the issue of this document does not imply that you will accept the lowest priced, or any tender'. In other words just because you ask for a quote does not mean that you have to buy anything. You should also make it clear that any costs incurred in bidding are to be met by the supplier and that you are not liable for any expenses they incur from bidding etc.

WRITING STYLE AND SKILLS

Style

The journalists motto is 'Make it smart, make it snappy, make it up!'. The last of these is not advised but keeping things short and simple is highly recommended. The less scope for misunderstanding and confusion the better.

George Orwell provided general guidance on writing in his six elementary rules. From the essay *Politics and the English Language,* George Orwell offered the following 'six elementary rules' for writers:

(i) Never use a metaphor, simile or other figure of speech that you are used to seeing in print.

(ii) Never use a long word when a short one will do.

(iii) If it is possible to cut out a word, always cut it out.

(iv) Never use the passive voice when you can use the active.

(v) Never use a foreign phrase, a scientific word or a jargon word if you can think of an everyday English equivalent.

(vi) Break any of these rules sooner than say anything outright barbarous.

Although he was talking about both creative writing and journalism it does make sense for any writing and the rewrite of this advice provided in Table 5.7 should be of help.

TABLE 5.7   *Orwell's six elementary rules for writers*

Orwell's guidance	Example or comment
Never use a metaphor, simile or other figure of speech that you are used to seeing in print.	Say 'now' rather than 'at this moment in time' etc.
Never use a long word when a short one will do.	It is very popular at the moment is to say 'utilise' instead of 'use'.
If it is possible to cut out a word, always cut it out.	Keep in mind the journalist's motto: make it sharp, make it snappy, make it up!
Never use the passive voice when you can use the active	In other words say 'John read the book' not 'The book was being read by John'. The main reason for this is that it is easier to understand, but it also cuts down on the number of words: always a good thing.
Never use a foreign phrase, a scientific word or a jargon word if you can think of an everyday English equivalent	In the air traffic control business they talk about 'bandstanding' when they mean operating a single runway for both landing and take-off unlike at a major airport where you would usually have two, one for landings and the other for take-offs. For a non-specialist audience just say 'using one run way for arrivals and departures'.

(Continued)

TABLE 5.7 *(Continued)*

Orwell's guidance	Example or comment
Break any of these rule sooner than say anything outright barbarous	Exercise for the reader or writer. Read what you have written and see for yourself.

KEY POINT

Read anything you have written aloud (in private if you prefer). If it does not sound right then it is almost certainly not right; this is a good way of checking Orwell's last dictum.

Corporate style

For those seeking training and guidance for this type of writing then the Plain English Society (see the list of organisations at the end of the book) is a good first step. There are also organisations that provide writing services and training, a search of the web is useful here; of course the author can also advise.

KEY POINT

What you write and submit to suppliers will give a strong impression of what your organisation is like to deal with. A badly constructed, poorly presented document will give a similar impression. Keep in mind that suppliers are potential partners and how you come across to them matters. They may even become your customers, so put in the effort to do a good job.

Approach

Producing large documents can be daunting to those whose job does not include writing on a regular basis. One solution to this is to hire an appropriately skilled author to help; you may know one or you can try agencies, local business and so on. If you do not want to do this (it can be expensive) then the following advice will help.

This short section offers a few hints and tips on writing style and approach for supplier documents. It has been assumed that you are writing in English for someone whose first language is also English. If this is not the case then you need to err further on the side of simplicity. Table 5.8 provides some pointers.

TABLE **5.8**   *Pointers for writing supplier documents*

Item	Guidance
Apostrophes	A minefield, but the grossest errors concern the following: its (belonging to it); it's (it is).
Diagrams, figures and tables	Use them where they make things clearer (and save you words); always give them a title and a reference.
Format	Use a simple layout, include page number and date on every page, use easily readable font in a sensible size (e.g. Arial or Times New Roman in 11 point). Set margins so that there is space for the reader to make notes. Use single-sided printing, unless you are producing large documents or many copies in which case save paper by using double.
KISS	Stands for 'keep it simple, stupid': do not make things complicated if you can avoid it; be clear and concise.
Lists	If you need a list of required items then either bullet them or, often better, number the items for ease of reference. Clarity is the goal.
Paragraph	Only have one topic in a paragraph.
Punctuation	Keep this simple too: as a minimum sentences start with a capital letter and end with a full stop; try not to need more than two commas in between.
Sentence length	Try to keep sentences at less than 20 words.
Sentence structure	Keep it simple; do not have lots of subclauses and conditional statements.
Vocabulary	Avoid jargon where possible; never use a longer word or phrase where there is a shorter one.

KEY POINT

The Plain English Society offers online guides for free and training courses for those wishing to get help with the effective use of English.

LOOKING AFTER IT ALL

It may be boring, but the bottom line is that you should keep copies of everything you send out and everything you receive.

KEY POINT

Electronic copies will suffice, but make sure you keep them backed up to somewhere you can (i) easily get them back from and (ii) be sure they are safe. Many SMEs have IT backup facilities that are seldom tested; you may think the information is safe, but is it and can you get it back?

It is also useful to keep a log or register of what you sent out, to whom and when and what you received, from whom and when. This can then form the basis of an index for filing so you can quickly retrieve anything you need. Being organised will make the procurement that much easier.

Table 5.9 gives an example template you can use. It can be expanded to suit your needs; you might wish to specify physical or logical locations or file names and so on.

TABLE **5.9**   *Example template for keeping track of documents*

Document	Sent to	When	Receipt from	Response received from
RFI	ABC, DEF, GHI	23/11/01	ABC, 24/11/01 DEF, 25/11/01 GHI, 24/11/01	ABC DEF

SUMMARY

Unless it is for something trivial there is likely to be a fair amount of paper and electronic material relating to any IT procurement. Creating this and looking after it can be a significant parcel of work, particularly for an SME that is less likely to have specialists in-house who do this all of the time. It is important to understand the amount of effort and administration that can go with this; a bespoke IT procurement is a significant undertaking in this respect. The templates and examples in this chapter can give you a sound starting point, but you may need to consider outside help from a technical author if you do not have the internal resources to cope.

6 Bid Evaluation

Here we cover the identification of selection criteria: it is not just price. We describe making evaluation models (spreadsheets), reporting on evaluations, decision makers and advisers, financial concerns, lifecycle versus upfront costs (e.g. software licences, leasing versus purchase and so forth) and TCO.

INTRODUCTION

Hopefully by this point you have identified what you want and have provided potential suppliers with enough information to fulfil that need. The next step is to select the supplier(s) that will give you the best outcome. The word outcome has been chosen here as it is not just a matter of price, performance and service, but also a holistic treatment of everything that relates to your business or organisational requirement. In order to make this selection it is necessary to evaluate the offerings of the different suppliers. This chapter gives some suggestions and processes that can be adapted to help make this choice.

The areas covered here include establishing an approach or programme, establishing criteria, client communications, negotiation and change, evaluating submissions and final approval.

KEY POINT

The majority of this chapter is aimed at the more complex end of the IT procurement spectrum that an SME might be involved in; you would not expect to have evaluation teams if you are just buying a new mouse in a two-person business. A short section at the end covers consumables and other small procurements.

APPROACH

The first thing to keep in mind is that it is not just price. Many SMEs have made appalling errors by making their choice with price as the first, or only, decision criteria.

The suggestion here, and it is based on a simplified version of approaches taken for major procurements, is to adopt a three-stage process. In the first stage the no-hopers are eliminated: those who are way out on price or obviously do not understand what you want. It is essentially a triage approach where you target the effort where it is most effective.

The second stage involves evaluating the remaining suppliers against some basic criteria and getting down to a shortlist of three or four; if you are lucky there may be a clear winner visible already. However, it may still be worth looking at a couple of others to give you more comparison and to build confidence in the decision.

The final stage covers detailed assessment of each bid (you do not want to do this for every bid as it would take too much time).

CRITERIA

To support the evaluation you need to decide what criteria to base your decision on. These will come in two main categories: quantitative and qualitative. The former are easier to deal with than the latter, although the trick with the qualitative criteria is to put them into some sort of form that you can measure. Thus making them something that you can easily compare, the Holy Grail is to be able to compare like with like. However, it is worth noting that in some cases allocating scores to criteria can be a value judgement: this makes them somewhat qualitative. For this reason there may be some difference of opinion as to which criteria should be in which category. As long as all of those engaged in the procurement agree this does not matter, the goal is to help you make a supportable and, hopefully, rational decision.

An important point to consider is that whatever criteria are chosen, they should reflect what is important to you and your business. For example if finances are very tight then you may want to put price above all but the basic, essential functions. If your biggest need is to improve the service you deliver to your clients because they are expressing dissatisfaction with how long it takes you to process an order, then price may be secondary (within reason).

> **KEY POINT**
>
> These criteria should be consistent with those you specified when defining your needs and those you may have communicated to the suppliers in earlier stages. There is no point in evaluating the proposals against irrelevant criteria.

Quantitative criteria

Although there may be quite a few of these they have the benefit of being things you can measure. Hopefully you will have identified most of these when establishing your original business needs. However, as a result of communication with the suppliers and their subsequent proposals you may have new criteria or change those you started with.

The aim is to get enough criteria defined to make an impartial and informed view as to which supplier has the best offering (even if you then choose another for non-quantitative reasons). You should look at having a relatively small range of values for scoring these; points out of 5 seems to be quite useable, less than 3 gets too coarse and more than 10 can be misleading and subjective.

You can use these criteria for relative scoring, to choose who is the best in that area. You can also use them as absolute accept or reject filters. For example you may choose to eliminate any supplier that has a poor recent financial track record or has not been trading for at least three years.

The following sections describe common quantitative criteria that you can consider as a starting point. Note that these are given in business requirements terms.

Performance

This can be measured in terms of:

(i) how long it takes to do something (e.g. to process an order, check on stock availability, process a credit card transaction, calculate a price);

(ii) how much does the system need to deal with at any given time (e.g. how many simultaneous users a system must support, how many items it must be able to track at one time and so forth).

Capacity

Capacity is typically measured in terms of:

(i) what volume of information needs to be accommodated (e.g. how many customer records do you need to keep, how many stock items must the system be able to store);

(ii) what volume of information must be stored short term and long term (e.g. available 'instantly' within an hour, same day, within a week from offsite archive storage).

Availability

This is measured in terms of how much of the time the service or equipment is working as required. Specified in terms of a percentage in a given time. A target that is then met, exceeded or not met. Has a sometimes significant impact on cost. Figures need to take into account scheduled maintenance, time to repair faults and equipment to cover whilst faults are fixed.

Price

The price is not always as easy to measure as you might think. Consider:

(i) capital costs;

(ii) recurrent costs (in particular repeat licence fees);

(iii) warranty period included (it may be cheaper to exclude it thereby gaining a discount and use existing maintenance arrangements);

(iv) leasing costs, credit charges and similar;

(v) TCO over the working life of a service or product.

See also the later section on financial evaluation.

Timetable

Can they meet your timetable? If not do they offer a good reason (i.e. something you have not allowed for, because you did not know about it or forgot to include it)?

Project or service management

If you are procuring anything that is bespoke or tailored to your needs (and this can be just having hardware installed at your site) then you should know how they go about running projects and managing progress in general.

Quality (assurance)

Do they have a QA system? What accreditation do they have? What are your minimum requirements for this? If they do not have a formal QA system what processes do they have in place to make sure you get what you order? For example even if you are just buying a printer they should have some form of goods return process. How do they support warranties and process warranty claims? Do they have established QA for the supply chains that they use, e.g. for people, good and services? How do they guarantee security of supply? See Chapter 7 for details of QA requirements.

Financial track record

Are they financially viable, at least for the period of your procurement and any post-delivery support and warranty? Ideally this should be longer as you do not really want to have to keep looking for new suppliers.

Company reputation

Also covered as a qualitative criterion, in this case the question is whether they have any outstanding legal disputes with existing or previous clients. If so, what is being done to resolve them? In the latter case you should establish whether these are a threat to the viability of the supplier. Note that most organisations will have disputes from time to time and it is not always an indicator that a supplier is not good, but it is important to make this a conscious decision.

Service and delivery track record

They should be able to provide you with evidence where they have done this or similar work before and give you references that you can follow up.

The quality of this can be scored by comparison with the other suppliers or in absolute terms if you wish to set a minimum criterion.

Flexibility (solution)

Consider how flexible the product, solution or service offering is in terms of your business needs. It can include:

(i)   growth and scalability in capacity;
(ii) growth and scalability in performance;
(iii) configurability;
(iv) ability to cope with change (during and after development);
(v)   upgrade path for applications and new functionality;
(vi) implementation in stages not just 'big bang';
(vii) expansion to new sites and so forth.

There will be a trade-off against cost, but flexibility may be an indication of the long-term value of investment. As a minimum it must be flexible enough to support the business case for the procurement.

Capability

Do they have the breadth and depth of knowledge and resources needed to take on and deliver the job you want done? For instance a local four-person firm may not have sufficient spare capacity to cover sick leave; this may be an issue if delivery is time critical for your business.

Added value

Are there any measurable added value items outside the scope of your specifications that are worthy of recognition? For example they may be willing to provide free software upgrades to deal with the effect of any operating system patches that occur within the next two years of use. They may be able to offer you discounts for trialling or testing software upgrades (although you may wish to balance this against risk to service).

Subcontractors

Where a supplier has to use subcontractors, for example for network cabling, what scores in relevant categories can you apply to them? Do they have established supply chain processes that relate to this?

KEY POINT

You need to be able to give a numerical score to any of these criteria: if you cannot then they are not quantitative. You may find that you have to do this iteratively; until you have looked at all of the answers you may not know what is a high or low score and the range of scores you want to use.

Qualitative criteria

It would be nice if there were no qualitative criteria but, particularly for an SME, these will matter. You may well have assessed that Company A is a bit cheaper, but if you cannot stand their project manager then you have to decide whether you can really work with them in the long term. We describe some common qualitative criteria in the following sections.

Management approach

How do they go about running their projects, dealing with clients and managing you as an account? For larger projects and long-term relationships you may want more of a partnership approach than that of customer–supplier.

Professionalism

This is related to the management approach, but more general and covering lower-level elements. Do they always do the following:

(i)   Respond in a timely manner?
(ii) Return phone calls and emails?
(iii) Correctly set expectations for what is going to happen?
(iv) Communicate any changes effectively?
(v)   Behave courteously?
(vi) Keep appointments?
(vii) Meet their own deadlines?

In summary do they give you a professional service and do they operate consistently and efficiently?

Company credibility

Are they seen as a market leader, a known brand or a long-established organisation within their market sector? Are they known for sustainable growth, good employment practices, having a good reputation for environmental and social impact?

Flexibility (organisation)

Some organisations will only work in one particular way. This may not be a problem; for example a PC supplier may only follow one process for choosing and delivering your system. In other cases they may expect you to change your business to suit them; for example they may only carry out installations at specific times etc. If you feel you may need flexibility then you should look for evidence of where they have adapted their services to suit their clients' needs.

Subcontractors and third parties

Can they do the job or provide the goods and services themselves or do they have to subcontract? If they use third parties what is their reputation for managing them effectively (see also the quantitative measure on this).

Comfort or relationship

Are you happy with the people you have met and will have to work with to implement what you are buying? This can be a purely subjective factor; if you do not like someone you may not want to risk that clouding your judgement when you work or are in conflict with them. For an existing supplier you will have the benefit of an existing relationship. Unless this is so bad that you have already decided not to deal with them again there will be good points and bad points to consider. It is helpful to keep in mind that because you know them better you may have more negative information than you have from the competitors. Do not be tempted to mark them down because of this or to take the other extreme of 'the devil you know'. Instead ask questions to try and benchmark the competitors against these strengths and weaknesses.

Relative size

Companies often get on better when they trade with similar sized organisations. In part this comes down to relative importance. Your £10,000 order is vital to you but relatively unimportant to a £1 billion turnover corporation (although it may matter to their local retail outlet; it is the turnover of the business unit that you are dealing with that matters most). On the other hand if you are placing a £50,000 order with a two-person firm it may represent too large a challenge to be low risk to you or them.

KEY POINT

Even qualitative criteria need to be measured; this may seem like a contradiction but unless you put some value against what may be just an impression, then you cannot make a comparison. Without a comparison there can be no evaluation: a paradox, but one that needs to be resolved. To be useful you will need to award some sort of score to your qualitative criteria.

Criteria for small procurements

For very small procurements it may not be worth investing much time in defining criteria, but you should at least consider price and reputation. So:

- get more than one quote: price is a criterion;
- choose suppliers by word of mouth, reputation or a known supplier: play it safe, quality is the criterion.

Scale and weighting

Once you have identified all of your criteria (you can always add more or remove some later if things change) you need to decide how you are going to score them. There are two points to this, scale and weighting.

As it makes sense to keep things as simple as possible you should adopt a simple scale. The author suggests that you adopt a range of 1 to 5 (or 1 to 3); in this 1 is seen as a poor score and 5 (or 3) is seen as a perfect score. This leaves you the option to use 0 as a totally unsatisfactory response or an eliminator. When using a range of 1 to 5, you might choose to make 3 a satisfactory answer, 4 an answer that exceeds requirements and 5 an innovative answer that would transform your ability to do business in some way. Examples of criteria you might use to apply scores are given in Table 6.1.

TABLE 6.1   *Example criteria to apply scores to suppliers*

Score	Comment
0	No response or totally non-compliant with requirements; not capable of being improved to meet needs.
1	Response provided meets only a small fraction of what is needed; not easily seen as capable of remedy by supplier to meet needs.
2	Less than compliant but capable of meeting minimum requirements if additional work done.
3	Minimum acceptable response; compliant with what is needed.
4	Shows benefits over and above the baseline requirement.
5	An exceptional response that offers a revolutionary or significant improvement over what was thought practical.

Not all criteria are equal. Some are more equal than others; you resolve this by allocating a weighting to the different criteria. Giving thought to how you rank the different criteria will help you get an overall assessment biased towards what you need most. Again it is suggested that you weight on a scale of 1 to 5 with an appropriate factor that you multiply the score by. The values given in Table 6.2 are examples; you should make up weights that you are comfortable with. You do not need to have this many, feel free to simplify if you do not require this level of complexity: do not do work that you do not need to.

TABLE 6.2   *Example weights and factors applied to criteria*

Weight	Description	Factor
1	Entirely optional and has no impact on the ability to meet business needs or has limited additional value (e.g. aesthetic appearance of a report)	30%
2	Needed for ease of use, 'would be nice' etc.; minor additional benefit	50%
3	Not essential but adds significant value to service	70%
4	Important; if not included then service is degraded	80%
5	Vital; an absolute must have	100%

Another factor that you can consider is the balance between the technical, financial and management aspects of the procurement. You might choose to give 60% of the weighting for the solution and meeting requirements, 10% for their management approach and 30% for the price. The worked spreadsheet example in the evaluating submissions section below shows how you can do this.

COMMUNICATION

Internally

When you are evaluating bids it is important that everyone involved within your organisation knows what criteria, the basis for your decision, are being used. Partly this is so that you score the responses against a common set of requirements, comparing like with like. It is possibly more important that you can check that you agree on the criteria that are to be used.

With the suppliers

There is a school of thought that you should keep the basis of your decision criteria secret from suppliers so that they do not just say what you want to hear. There is some merit in this. However, you do want the suppliers to give you what you need, so keeping them entirely in the dark turns it into a guessing game. This can waste everyone's time.

EVALUATING SUBMISSIONS

The Holy Grail of evaluation is to arrive at a position where you can accurately compare like with like. Even very experienced procurement teams can find this difficult, frequently having to ask supplementary questions, conduct further interviews and so forth before they arrive at a verdict. Having a scoring system that you can apply equally to all suppliers who bid or quote helps.

KEY POINT

The important thing to keep in mind with evaluation is that all decision makers need to agree with the method used. It is pointless going through an evaluation exercise, using up your valuable time, and then having someone else decide to do something else altogether. Call them decision makers, stakeholders or what you like: an evaluation needs to involve and be acceptable to all.

Scoring models

There are many ways to score a proposal, you can make it as simple or as complicated as you wish. You can have multiple criteria, weighted scores, weighted pricing elements, independent assessors and specialist teams and so on and so on. However in this book the aim is to provide something practical for the SME.

First Cut Evaluation	Score - 0 to 4			
Company	**Bloggo**	**Priceybutgood**	**Pricey**	**Cheap**
COSTS				
Equipment	3	3	2	4
Installation	2	3	1	4
Annual Support	3	3	1	3
SubTotal	8	9	4	11
REQUIREMENTS				
Must Have	4	4	4	3
Would Like	3	3	3	2
Added Value	2	2	1	0
Bonus Features	0	1	0	0
SubTotal	9	10	8	5
CREDIBILITY				
Implementation Plan	3	4	3	2
Processes/QA	3	4	4	0
Technical Ability	4	4	3	2
Reputation	3	3	2	2
Relationship	4	3	2	2
Staff	3	4	2	2
Sub total	20	22	16	10
Total	**37**	**41**	28	26
Pass mark set at	**30**			

Note: Costs based on relative ranking, however, anyone outside average by more than 50% eliminated.

FIGURE 6.1 *Basic evaluation spreadsheet*

Figure 6.1 shows a snapshot of a simple spreadsheet for evaluating the purchase of a desktop publishing system. Four suppliers quoted (Bloggo, Priceybutgood, Pricey and Cheap). Of these both Bloggo and Priceybutgood were existing suppliers. The scoring system was from 0 to 4, with a filter built in to stop people buying (i.e. quoting an unrealistically, unsustainably low price) the business or being considered if widely outside the core range of pricing.

From this it can be seen that on price, flexibility and solution fit, the two were within a few points of each other. However, the overall working relationship with Bloggo and other 'qualitative' factors gave them the edge. Note that these 'soft' factors still had to be scored.

To choose between the two, each was asked to deliver a presentation based on their proposed solution or offering. Before this they were supplied with key questions based on the perceived strengths and weaknesses of their respective proposals.

Based on the presentation the scores were revised; in this case the small advantage shown by Bloggo increased and they were awarded the business.

KEY POINT

The easiest way to implement an evaluation model is on a spreadsheet. If you have nobody in-house who can do this (unlikely these days) and it is an issue, your local office temp agency could provide you with the expertise. The cost will be worth it compared with paper, pencil and calculator.

Another method

In the example finance has simply been dealt with as another criterion. Another approach is to split the proposal or bid into two distinct components that are evaluated separately then merge their scores at the end of the process. This is useful where the financial elements are particularly complex and require a specialist team to make the comparison. However, this is an unlikely situation for SMEs. If you do adopt this method then you need to decide how important each overall element is, then award percentages to each accordingly. For example you may decide that price is worth 40% and the rest (sometimes called the 'quality response'; not to be confused with QA) worth 60%.

Financial evaluation

We touched on the financial points in both the business case and when identifying the business needs themselves in Chapter 3. As with the scoring models a spreadsheet is the right tool for the job. Table 6.3 lists factors that you might need to consider when putting together a financial model.

TABLE 6.3 *Factors to consider when putting together a financial model*

Factor	Comments
Capital cost	The simplest element of the price: what do the raw materials or equipment and other capital cost? It should be easy to make this a like for like comparison between the different suppliers. Make sure that they have a shopping list table to fill in, e.g. 10 laser printers, £X. These are charges that count as capital on your balance sheet.
Cash flow	Simply what it costs you to finance the purchase yourself versus any income it might generate: effectively the cost of borrowing.
One-off charges	For example installation charges, training costs or anything else that is a one-off, non-capital charge.
Recurrent costs	These include periodic charges, e.g. for renewable licences, consumables, maintenance and so forth.
Penalty and reward clauses	Where you have a service contract with a supplier there may be penalty charges where the supplier fails to meet the agreed contract (probably termed a service level agreement (SLA)). These may be in the form of discounts against future payments or lump sum repayments. You can compare the offerings of the different suppliers.
Service charges and ad hoc fees	Charges for annual or monthly support etc. One-off fees based on specific events, such as call-out charges for onsite maintenance visits.
Payment schedules	The payment schedule can make a significant difference to your cash flow and confidence in the supplier. For instance supplier A may ask for 50% in advance, 30% on completion of the software and the balance, 20%, on acceptance. Supplier B may ask for 25% upfront, 35% on completion, 20% on acceptance and 20% after 30 days successful operation. Both in terms of cash flow and not paying until you are sure it works gives the vote to supplier B.
Cost of finance	Specifically those made by the supplier, e.g. for leasing rather than buying the equipment, rental versus ownership, buy-back options on old equipment and so forth.
Time and materials	Daily rates and margins on purchased materials not covered in the main delivery. For example a supplier might say that additional IT consultancy can be purchased at £Y per day.
TCO	Cost of the service or product over its complete working life; you may have to calculate this based on the information supplied and forecasts, e.g. for inflation etc.
Validity	How long the bid is valid for: a short period such as a week or a month may not fit with your decision-making plan or timetable. If the validity is less than you asked for then you may choose to reject it.

Figure 6.2 shows a simple financial evaluation spreadsheet. In this very basic example one supplier offers a capital cost for the equipment, the other a lease cost. A simple finance charge has been included for the

purchase option. In the case of Bloggo there is just a support cost per year; it has been assumed that the equipment has a residual value after five years of just 10% of the new cost. In many cases for IT this would be optimistic; it may easily be worthless if sold, although it might continue to be of use in-house. This takes no account of tax relief, depreciation etc. but attempts to show that leasing will have a different cost profile to purchase; in this case over the short term the lease is much better, over the longer term things are more equal.

Company		PURCHASE	LEASE
		Bloggo	Priceybutgood
Equipment Cost		24,500	0
Cost of Finance 3 yrs (10% pa)		7,350	1,500
Support/Lease Y1		1,000	5,000
Support/Lease Y2		1,000	5,000
Support/Lease Y3		1,000	5,000
Residual Value Y3		10,000	0
Network Upgrade at Y3		3,000	0
Support/Lease Y4		1,200	6,500
Support/Lease Y5		1,200	6,500
Cost of finance Y3–5 (10% pa)		4,900	1,200
Residual Value Y5		2,450	0
TCO 3 Years		24,850	16,500
TCO 5 Years		31,500	30,700
NOTE - No allowance for depreciation has been made here.			

FIGURE 6.2   *Simple financial example*

Things are more complex in the real world: there are leasing and licensing charging regimes to consider, service charges, technology refreshes and the like, not to mention tax considerations. Here a more sophisticated approach is needed. The reader is directed to *Finance for IT Decision Makers: A Practical Handbook for Buyers, Sellers and Managers* by Blackstaff (2006).

Evaluation teams

Unless only a single person is involved in evaluating the submissions from suppliers then it is a team exercise. This implies an evaluation team or board etc.

Such a panel needs to have the relevant skills needed to make a sensible comparison of the proposals received. They also need the skills necessary to ask suppliers questions to fill in the gaps that are inevitable with any procurement exercise.

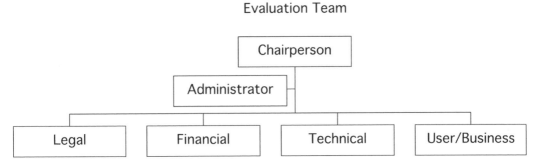

FIGURE 6.3 *Structure of the evaluation team*

Figure 6.3 shows a possible structure for an evaluation team. Table 6.4 looks at these roles and skills in a little more detail. It is often necessary in an SME to have one person performing more than one of these roles. Some people may only be consulted as and when needed. In some cases the panel is just one person.

TABLE 6.4 *Roles and skills of the evaluation team*

Role	Comments
Chairperson	Keeps order in the meetings and makes sure things follow an agenda.
Administrator	Records any minutes and actions as needed.
Legal	Provides legal advice, in particular relating to T&Cs and other contractual matters.
Financial	Provides a financial assessment of the proposal; must understand the impact of accepting a proposal on the business in the short and long term.
Technical expert	Able to understand the more technical elements, for example must be able to say whether it will meet your storage and processing needs initially and as forecast. In the case of organisations that have to meet specific standards (e.g. for quality accreditation), more than one 'expert' may be needed.
User/Business need	Someone who represents the views of those who will actually make use of the equipment or system. They need not be technical but must be able to assess to what extent the needs of the business and those who are going to use it will be met.

KEY POINT

Everyone on this panel needs to be able to explain what they do to the others.

Recommendation

Once the panel has completed the evaluations it then either makes the decision itself or passes on a recommendation to the person who does (in the case of the S end of the SME market the panel is likely to be small and make the decision). There are likely to be only four outcomes, as detailed in Table 6.5.

TABLE 6.5 *The four likely recommendations of the evaluation team*

Recommendation	Comments
Do nothing or No winner	None of the bids met your needs in a way that supports the business case (this is why you have a disclaimer that you may choose not to award, bid at your own cost etc.). This may be down to price, poor responses or major shortcomings.
Clear winner	One supplier is out in front by a big enough margin. The best outcome for all concerned. You have a bid that supports the business case with a supplier you trust.
Marginal winner	Too close to call: maybe the winner is better in more areas than the next best, but they are still worse in some areas. You might choose to award it to the winner, subject to them improving their offering to remedy their shortcomings. You can keep the second place as a standby (be honest) in case your winner cannot do this at a realistic price. Messy but does happen.
Clarification	You do not have enough information to make the decision; this may be your own fault (poor specification) or the suppliers (poor responses). Whatever the reason you need to ask for more information.

FINAL APPROVAL

Ultimately somebody has to carry the can for the decision and has to authorise payment. How this happens varies from organisation to organisation; for the sole trader or small partnership it is straightforward. At the larger end of the spectrum there may be a requirement for more than one person to agree. These people will (perhaps should) have been part of the procurement plan. In cases where they were not part of the evaluation process then there will need to be a presentation of the recommendation for final approval. This can range from a chat over a cup of tea through to a formal presentation to the board with accompanying documentation. Make sure this is planned for and that suppliers are aware of any delays that may result.

If the recommendation is rejected then it is up to the decision makers to decide what to do next. Keep in mind that for anything but small proposals the supplier has incurred significant cost: they may refuse to bid in the future if you mess them about without good reason.

CONSUMABLES AND LOW-VALUE ITEMS

The material that precedes this section is concerned with the more complex procurements where, for example, you are buying a bespoke solution. It would be far too time-consuming and expensive to adopt such an approach for buying low-value items or small volumes of consumables.

However, you may still need to make comparisons even when you are buying something small. The thing to keep in mind is that you must always compare like with like. For example if you are buying paper then the weight (how heavy or thick the paper is, measured in grams per square metre; photocopy paper is 80 gsm), applications (inkjet, laser, photocopier or universal), colour and finish (normal, photographic, glossy, matt etc.) are all factors to consider. Any price comparison would need to take these into account. Similarly the quantity you have to commit to would come into it. You might get a better price on eight boxes of paper than on one pack of 500 pages, but if it takes you a year to get through this much then you are effectively losing notional interest in money tied up in your stock of paper.

Of course if you are buying a huge quantity of low-volume items then the large financial cost will merit you treating it as a serious procurement exercise.

KEY POINT

Spend only as much time as is justified in making the like for like comparison for low-value items.

SUMMARY

Next to determining what you want in the first place (needs analysis), evaluating the bids or quotes you receive is the most important part of the procurement. Even if you are just getting a few quotes for a new PC you still need to make sure that you are comparing like with like and that what you are being offered will do the job. Following a simple process (there is no need for massive bureaucracy with formal meetings and tons of documentation) will help you make an informed evaluation. Making a rational choice based on sound reasoning significantly increases the chances of a successful outcome.

KEY POINT

However simple or complex the deal, you must aim to compare like with like or time spent on your evaluation will be wasted.

7 Quality Assurance

Here we describe QA applied to procurements: why and how etc. We also explain how to fit in with corporate QA, supplier QA requirements (i.e. what they must do) and quality standards.

INTRODUCTION

Owing to its title this chapter may not be the one that the reader turns to first; in many cases it may not be read at all. This is a pity as taking the QA elements of procurement seriously can help you get what you need. So it is not something to be cast aside because it seems a little dull. This chapter has been written to emphasise the elements and principles of QA that give quick wins and also to help the reader see that attention to this subject area is beneficial. The emphasis is on getting the benefits with the minimum of additional administration.

WHAT IS QA?

A familiar early example of QA is the hallmark system used on precious metals such as gold and silver in the UK since 1327 (although the London Goldsmiths' Company has been hallmarking since as early as 1300). Assay offices checked the gold or silver content of items and then stamped a mark to show that they met required levels of precious metal content: the hallmark.

At the time of writing Wikipedia, the internet encyclopaedia that some say lacks any QA itself, defined it as follows:

> Quality Assurance is the activity of providing evidence needed to establish confidence among all concerned, that the quality-related activities are being performed effectively. All those planned or systematic actions necessary to provide adequate confidence that a product or service will satisfy given requirements for quality. Quality Assurance is a part and consistent pair of quality management proving fact-based external confidence to customers and other stakeholders that products meet needs, expectations, and other requirements. QA (quality assurance) assures the existence and effectiveness of procedures that attempt to make sure – in advance – that the expected levels of quality will be reached. (www.wikipedia.org)

The entry goes on to say that

> Quality Assurance (QA) covers all activities from design, development, production, installation, servicing and documentation. It introduced the sayings 'fit for purpose' and 'do it right the first time'. It includes the regulation of the quality of raw materials, assemblies, products and components; services related to production; and management, production, and inspection processes. (www.wikipedia.org)

This latter focus on assemblies, products and components is where it becomes relevant to procurement.

So far, so good. Sadly once it gets going QA can turn into a bureaucratic nightmare. If you are not careful the quality plan and the work associated with it can exceed the rest of the procurement put together. The guiding principle is to keep in mind your original objective and keep things in proportion.

KEY POINT

Balance the benefits of QA with the amount of effort involved, beware going over the top.

PDCA: A QA PRINCIPLE

A review of QA literature will quickly identify the 'plan, do, check, act' (PDCA) approach. This seems to be the basis of most QA. This concept was championed by William Edwards Deming and Walter Shewhart. It came to prominence in the 1980s although both of them had been working towards it from the late 1930s. Figure 7.1 shows it in diagrammatic form. The key point is that it is a continual process, indeed the phrase 'continual improvement' has its roots in QA terminology. The idea is that by reviewing processes and outcomes versus objectives you can enter a virtuous circle.

FIGURE 7.1   *The QA PDCA diagram*

Table 7.1 shows how it is typically applied. For an SME it would be difficult to apply this to a single procurement, it is intended to support ongoing processes. If you want to benefit from this then you might wish to consider having a general procurement process for your business; this would then evolve over time: it would apply equally to all procurements, including IT.

TABLE 7.1 *Application of PDCA*

Plan	Do	Check	Act
Assess risks, identify processes needed, define processes to meet needs, identify objectives and outcomes	Document processes, train staff in use of processes, record keeping etc.	Review performance against the processes	Take remedial action based on non-conformance with reviews, consider process improvements

QA IN SMES

The question is why have QA at all (but that is for somebody else's book to answer, some examples are listed in the references and further reading)? Off-the-cuff answers include, 'because my clients insist that their suppliers have QA accreditation', 'because we are an engineering firm', 'because we see real benefits from having QA', 'we supply QA services so have to practice what we preach' etc. Some say, 'because it saves us money in wasted effort, and helps deliver a better service to our clients', but not as many as you might hope.

The history of QA standards such as the British BS 5750 (effectively the ISO 9000 series) has its roots in armaments factories in WWI. Too many explosions were happening and a checking system to make sure that people performed the correct (safe) actions repeatedly was developed with happy results. Many other safety critical applications followed similar routes; the aircraft industry springs to mind where critical work is always checked by a third party, that is independently inspected and a record is kept to see what has been done and checked. This is a major contribution to the first-rate safety record of the aircraft industry. Since then QA has spread into almost all areas of business.

The author's entirely ad hoc and unrepresentative research seemed to show that the smaller the SME the less likely they are to have QA unless it is thrust upon them. In the 1990s there was some, possibly equally ad hoc, research that showed that amongst FTSE 500 companies those with ISO 9000 style accreditation (BS 5750 was referred to at the time) were more likely to go out of business than those without. At that time this may have been because the cost of implementing outweighed the benefits of having it and many implementations were clumsy. But it was an interesting statistic for the author to tease the QA manager with when he was involved with putting in ISO 9000. At that time the main goal of QA systems was repeatability, not necessarily business improvement. Contemporary QA standards are building in elements of process improvement along with the more traditional audit trail style of QA. It can be more than a passive assurance overhead.

However QA is becoming increasingly popular in SMEs. This is underlined by the existence of a British Standards Institution website for Small Business Support (see www.bsi-global.com/en/ Standards-and-Publications/How-we-can-help-you/Business/Small-Businesses/).

From the point of view of this book the reality is that you either have it or you do not. If you do it will affect your procurement, but you will have someone responsible for the QA system that can help. This may be an internal or an external resource; if external there may be a cost to be incurred in getting that advice. If you do not have QA then you do not need to worry, but it might be worth taking on board some of the principles if this is a critical procurement for you.

KEY POINT

QA requirements are often cascaded down through the supply chain; this can mean that both the SME and its suppliers come within the QA net.

WHY HAVE ANY QA FOR AN SME PROCUREMENT?

As discussed above this may be thrust upon you, in which case you have to do what is required. Your QA expert or department should be able to tell you what to do and you then need to include it and plan for it. Even if you do not have to have QA there are certain QA-related activities that are of benefit to any procurement, whether you call them QA or not. For example just having an internal review of your procurement documents by someone other than the author(s) will reduce the number of errors and give you a critical view. Essentially this is a QA activity even if that is not what you call it.

As was mentioned in the brief introduction to QA, the term 'fit for purpose' was coined to cover such work. Introducing elements of QA into your procurement activities will increase the chance of what you buy being 'fit for purpose' and will provide you with measures to identify whether suppliers provide you with equipment, materials or services that are not.

SLAs that form part of many IT contracts are essentially enforceable QA measures. If the supplier fails to meet the QA measure, for example response time to fix a fault, then there is often a financial penalty associated with it.

KEY POINT

With any QA system what you measure tends to be what you get. You need to make sure that you are measuring what is important; otherwise effort is focused on the wrong things.

Special QA requirements

In specialist industries and in organisations with formal QA procedures there may well be QA requirements that suppliers have to meet. For example in the aviation industry where parts are certified there will be accompanying paperwork. It would be essential to specify that all such paperwork is included and checked.

Similarly you may have specific QA needs: for example requiring your suppliers to have particular levels of accreditation that they have to meet in order for your QA auditors to maintain your own accreditation.

These needs will vary from organisation to organisation and it is outside the scope of this book to cover all of the possibilities. The main consideration is to document your QA needs before you ask the supplier to quote or bid.

KEY POINT

Specify any QA requirements you have of your suppliers early and completely. Telling them later on may cause them to drop out: they will either have it, be getting it soon or not.

SCOPING THE QA FOR AN SME PROCUREMENT

A significant factor in this is going to be the size of the procurement and whether or not it is more of a project than an administrative exercise. Try and keep any requirements focused on areas that are of direct benefit to you. For the suppliers these will typically include:

- certification and acceptance requirements for any materials, equipment and off-the-shelf software;
- standards for software development;
- standards and methods for project management;
- environmental standards;
- operational standards for security;
- operational standards for service delivery, availability and disaster recovery etc.
- metrics for services and support.

For your internal processes they may include:

- documentation sign off and approval;
- audit of standards placed on suppliers (see the previous list);
- supplier approval processes;
- documentation audit trails.

Of course if your organisation has QA processes in place for projects then a significant procurement, as it is a project, will probably come within its scope. If you have a QA department or manager they will be able to advise you here.

Questions to ask include the following:

- What parts of the procurement matter most?
- What quality standards do you have to meet internally?
- What quality standards do your clients require you to impose on your suppliers?
- What quality measures do you want your suppliers meet?
- How will you enforce them?

KEY POINT

Always ask 'What is the benefit of this?' when considering any QA requirement that you want the supplier to comply with.

Some common QA and other standards

Table 7.2 lists a few standards that you may come across with a brief note on their purpose.

TABLE 7.2 *Common QA and other standards*

Standard	Comments
ISO 9000 series	Quality Management (previously known in the UK as BS 5750). The most common QA standard (or set of standards) in Europe. Owes its distant origin to safety in munitions factories in WWI.
BS 7858:2004	Security Screening of Staff. Covers processes for identifying people who are unsuitable for specific roles or types of employment.

(Continued)

TABLE 7.2 (*Continued*)

Standard	Comments
BS 15000	IT Service Management. Supports the ITIL approach to 'best practice' for IT service (see below).
BS 7799 (ISO 27001)	Information Security. Covers both physical and IT security issues; you should expect anyone supplying you with data services to have some elements of this in place if they have your data in their hands.
ISO 14000 series	Environment Management. Looks at labelling, environmental management systems, lifecycle of products, risk assessment and so on. It can be integrated with ISO 18000 as part of an overall approach.
ISO 18000 series	Occupational Health and Safety (OHSAS). This standard deals with people at work and how you go about ensuring their safety. It is likely to affect your procurement where staff use the IT equipment you buy. For example how they go about using workstations, the way they sit, provision of eye tests, lighting and so forth. The goals of ISO 18000 are to minimise risk to employees and the public, to improve business performance and to help organisations to establish a responsible image.
PAS 99:2006	Publicly Available Specification 99 is an Integrated Management System designed to support the implementation of ISO 9001, ISO 14001, OHSAS 18001 etc. It covers: policy; planning; implementation and operation; performance assessment; improvement and management review. There are SME focused implementations of PAS 99.
ITIL	Information Technology Infrastructure Library. This gathers 'best practice' for all aspects of IT service management and delivery in a series of books. It covers provision of quality IT services, and the accommodation and environmental facilities needed to support IT. It is consistent with the BS 15000 series of service management standards.
ISPL	This is better established in Europe than in the UK. It largely originated in Holland, which is fortunate as it is available in English. It covers all aspects of IT procurement from strategy and planning through to risk management, tendering, contracts and decision making. It is probably overkill for many SME procurements but contains much that is useful as background for owners and managers.

NOTE

Specific industries (for example aviation, medical, railways, heavy engineering and so forth) have specific standards for QA and any IT you use in these industries will come within the scope of your accreditation. As this will be within your own area of expertise the author is assuming that you know about it.

QA measures on suppliers

If you have a formal QA system then it will specify what you need your suppliers to do and you simply pass this on to them. This may restrict your choice: a supplier without accreditation is unlikely to want to or be able to obtain accreditation within the time frame just for you. If you do not have any specific measures then it is up to you; you are free to choose anyone in the marketplace. However, you may still want to consider what QA processes they have in place.

To cope with the situations where suppliers do not have similar quality requirements to yourselves or necessary accreditations, many organisations have a supplier vetting process. Such a process will check things such as: financial viability; track record; customer references; quality systems and accreditation; human resource processes and policies; environmental and sustainability policies; and management structures and governance. This provides the basis for a QA checklist should you need one.

MINIMUM QA

As a minimum you should consider having QA processes for goods acceptance and rejection. Even if it is just replacement paper for a printer there should be a process that covers the following questions for anything you buy:

- Was the order authorised and are we expecting these goods?
- Did we place such an order?
- Is this what we ordered?
- Are all items present?
- Does it match the delivery note?
- Is it in the condition expected?
- Does it meet the QA requirements we specify?
- What do we do if there are problems with it?

KEY POINT

For procurement documents the QA will be underpinned by having the documents reviewed by representatives of all of those who will use or be affected by what is procured. At the very least get someone else to read anything you send out to a supplier.

SAMPLE QA PLAN CONTENTS

This section shows what to expect in a simple QA plan for a system or solution type of procurement. According to the OGC (the UK Government's guru on such matters) a project quality plan should contain the following items:

- Acceptance criteria: a prioritised list of criteria for the final product(s) that must be met before the customer will accept the final product(s).
- Quality responsibilities: who is responsible for each of the aspects of quality of the final product(s).
- Reference to any standards that need to be met.
- The quality control and audit processes to be applied to project management.
- Quality control and audit process requirements for specialist work.
- Change management procedures.
- Configuration management plan.
- Any tools to be used to ensure quality and their quality require-ments.
- Customer quality expectations and requirements.
- Organisational or programme quality management system and standards.
- Configuration management and change control requirements.

QA CHECKLIST

The following checklist is taken from the OGC 'Fitness for purpose' checklist (see www.ogc.gov.uk/documentation_and_templates_project_ quality_plan.asp) with additions by the author.

Does the plan clearly define ways in which you and
your customer's quality expectations will be met? ☐

Are the defined ways and methods sufficient
to achieve the required quality? ☐

Are responsibilities for quality defined up to
a level that is independent of the procurement
and procurement manager? ☐

Does the plan conform to any in-house
quality policy? ☐

Have you kept the paperwork to a minimum? ☐

Are there independent reviews for critical
documents? ☐

Have you checked your supplier for:

- accreditations; ☐
- references; ☐

- human resource policies (including compliance with employment law); ☐
- environmental policies; ☐
- financial status? ☐

SUMMARY

For many SMEs QA is not an issue for their procurements. That said anyone who has any sort of acceptance criteria that they apply before paying for goods and services has an embryo QA system by implication. For the SME, what is needed is the minimum of process and overhead necessary to help them obtain what they want. Where the SME's own customers require rigorous, perhaps accredited, QA procedures to be applied to procurement-related activities, it will be important to make sure that they are in place and auditable. This in turn may mean insisting on your suppliers having appropriate systems in place. The supply chain is often a component of a QA system. Those in safety critical industries will have specific QA needs and where IT is part of the delivered service it may require rigorous inspection and compliance regulation.

8 IT-specific Issues

Here we have specific sections on bulk hardware procurement, operating systems, desktop applications, software licence considerations, solutions, maintenance and support, helpdesks, IT processes and outsourcing (but not off shoring or complex strategies that are not relevant to SMEs).

INTRODUCTION

Much of this book is applicable to non-IT procurements, although the supporting examples and case studies have been taken from the target SME and IT audience. This chapter's purpose is to capture some of the issues that are related to IT and provide the reader (particularly readers who have limited IT knowledge) with pointers to help them succeed with their procurement.

In an ideal world this chapter would provide the IT novice with all of the information they need to be IT specialists able to complete every detail of their technical specifications and evaluate the responses. In fact when putting the proposal of this book together and when researching SMEs there were requests that the book should do this. Sadly the scope of doing this would produce a book that was greater than the sum of all of the other BCS books currently published and planned. So a more modest goal is to provide pointers and suggestions as to when and where to get help. You cannot know it all and with a good supplier you should not need to. What follows should be taken as an expanded glossary with hints and tips. Hopefully it will also act as a checklist of things to keep in mind for IT procurements; in particular do not forget training and maintenance.

TECHNOLOGY

For those who are not IT literate the thing to keep in mind is that IT does not do anything that you cannot do with a combination of pen, paper, shoeboxes and a cleft stick. It comes down to calculating, storing and communicating. IT just has the ability to do it faster, at a greater scale and with lots of jargon. Fortunately anyone under the age of 30 will have at least encountered IT at school and at work so are likely to have some idea of what is going on. In fact it is rare to find anyone under the age of 50 who does not use IT to some extent. In this book a passing familiarity with IT has been assumed.

Many people know how to use a PC either to access applications or to do office work. They will have some idea of what the various components in a PC do (memory, processor, disk, DVD, network connection and so forth).

This is not the same as understanding the technical implications of the performance of these components or the infrastructure you might need to support them.

However, when researching SMEs it was clear that some suppliers could mistake a little understanding for in-depth knowledge. It is very easy for a knowledgeable supplier to generate rafts of information that are meaningless to the SME business owner. The remedy to this is either to become an expert yourself or, better, stop them and make them explain in terms that you do understand. It can always be done in terms of shoeboxes, pen, paper and stretched string between tins cans when it comes down to it. It may take longer, but you should keep asking until they do explain in terms you can understand.

EXAMPLE

The author got roped in to help a friend of his wife who was publishing a book on Lulu (a publish-it-yourself community website, www.lulu.com). The person was a working non-IT-professional with basic IT skills. Underestimating how much more anyone with an IT background knows is very easy, the problem then being an incorrect assumption that others have the same level of skill. It is all too easy, as the author did, to start rabbiting on about JPEGs, TIFFs, bitmaps and compressed files only to discover the poor chap had no idea what was being discussed.

KEY POINT

Where the decision makers in an SME are non-technical it is vital that things are explained to them in terms that are readily understood.

What is in a personal computer?

One thing that came out of the research for this book was that not everyone knows what is in a PC (or a mobile phone for that matter); very few people know how they work but most of the time they do not need to, so it does not matter. Even if you are not going to be involved in the technical evaluation of what you buy it is useful to understand the basic vocabulary. This and the following section are there to help out. Figure 8.1 shows the basic components that you might find in a typical PC (this excludes peripherals such as speakers, webcams, external memory devices and the like) and a brief description is given in the following sections.

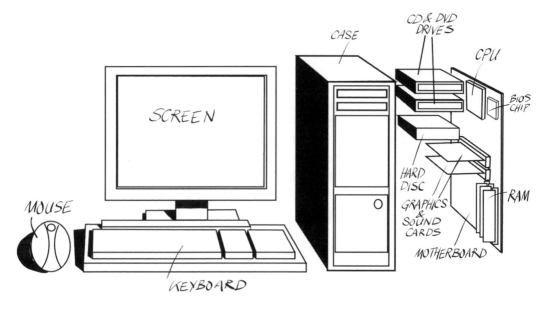

FIGURE 8.1   *Main PC components*

Central processor unit (CPU)

This is the part of the computer that 'thinks': it processes instructions that it gets from the RAM (that are loaded there from the program that is stored on a disk). Price depends on speed (some processors also have more than one CPU on them, for example dual core processors). Up to a certain point price will increase linearly with performance, after that it increases more rapidly; do not pay for this performance unless you really need it.

Random access memory (RAM)

This is the equivalent of a notebook where you do your working, take notes from meetings, put to do lists and so forth. This only stores information whilst the computer is running (for that reason it is sometimes called volatile storage). When you turn the computer off anything there is lost (this is why you need to 'save' things from time to time when working on a computer in case the power fails or someone pulls out the plug by mistake). This memory operates at 'high speed': it has to be fast enough to keep up with the CPU. The more RAM available and the faster it is the better.

Disk

A disk is a magnetic storage medium, essentially a fast spinning disk covered with an oxide layer that can store information magnetically. This operates at a slower speed than the RAM but provides long-term storage that is not lost when the machine is turned off. Programs and data are usually stored here. It is important to be able to backup this information to some other storage so that it is not lost if the disk or computer fails (or is stolen). As with RAM, the faster and large the disk the better: price will be the limiting factor.

Network adapter or card

Your computer talks to other local computers or the outside world via internal and external networks using this. A computer that is 'standalone' does not need this. It may be built into the 'motherboard' but is sometimes an optional extra. The adapter needs to be compatible with whatever hardware and software your network runs. You may need technical advice. Networks may be wired (with cabling) or wireless; there are different levels of performance and price relating to this. Usually wireless costs a little more, but the key price driver is speed (bandwidth).

Graphics adapter or card

The graphics card is a device that enables the computer to display information on a screen. It may have either analogue or digital output (also may be able to drive TV screens). It will have its own memory and processor. In general the more memory and faster the card the better. Up to a certain point the price is not an issue, but above that level (it changes all the time) there will be a steep increase in price. Only buy a fancy graphics card if you have a real need to and understand why you need it.

Basic input output system (BIOS)

We are getting technical here: the BIOS is what allows the PC to get going when you start it from cold. It uses some form of read only memory (ROM; although to add confusion this can often be rewritten or modified, see a computer dictionary for terms such as electronically programmable read only memory (EPROM)) to store the instruction the computer needs to talk to the disk and screen and get things going.

Sound card or audio adapter

This enables your computer to provide sound output to speakers and headphones and also to take in audio input from a microphone or other compatible sound source. Can be mono (rare) stereo or some form of surround sound. Power output and sound quality are the key features.

Motherboard

A motherboard connects everything together and provides the infrastructure for the major components; the graphics and sound adapters are often built in to this unit. The significant factor will be its performance and ability to support the other items; unless you are building your own unit from scratch this component will probably not affect your choice. The BIOS will be resident on the motherboard.

DVD or CD drive

This provides both a means of loading applications software and data from 'read only' optical media such as DVDs and compact discs (CDs) and a means of creating long-term storage. The advent of cheap DVD and CD drives that can create ('burn') DVDs and CDs with data on them from scratch has more or less condemned the floppy disk to history. The role of the floppy disk has also been taken over by the memory stick.

Monitor or display

This used to be a cathode ray tube (CRT) (original television technology) device, now more likely to be some form of flat screen technology. Key parameters are the viewable area (defined by a diagonal measurement), how small the dots are that make up the picture (resolution) and how quickly it can be updated. Price will reflect this.

Keyboard and mouse

The main consideration with a keyboard and mouse are their suitability for the job in hand. A machine used for a bit of light letter writing is not going to get the same level of use as a stock control machine in an industrial warehouse. The device needs to be specified appropriately for its intended use and environment. If you have a particularly coffee-careless operator an industrial liquid proof device may be justified in an office environment.

Power supply unit (PSU)

This should have sufficient power to cover any additional components you are likely to add such as extra disk drives and so forth.

NOTE

At the time of writing a 'run of the mill' PC would have at least 250 GB of disk space, 512 MB of RAM, a 2.0 GHz processor, a DVD read–write unit, a graphics card with 256 MB of memory, a surround sound audio adapter, a network adapter and a 17 inch flat screen monitor and cost about £350.

Terminology and metrics

The world of IT is filled with acronyms and abbreviations that can be confusing for the newcomer or those with limited knowledge. This short section provides some background on the alphabet soup of IT abbreviations and acronyms. It also provides some guidance on what they mean in the real world. It would have been possible to fill an entire book with this stuff and such books exist. However, this book is not intended as an IT primer or glossary and this sample is here for the genuinely baffled only. The explanatory notes are for the curious.

NOTE

Space dictates that this cannot be a comprehensive list, but it will help. Inevitably there will be those who say 'Why did you leave out this, that or the other?'. The answer is that something had to give.

Bit

This is a binary digit (1 or 0). It is the smallest piece of information in a computer memory (disk or otherwise), essentially a switch that is either on or off. It forms the basis of measuring how much and how fast for data: how many of them have you got room for and how many can you move from one place to another in a given time.

Byte

A byte is 8 bits of data. It boils down to the space you need to store one letter or number.

Kilobyte

As computers work in binary all numbers relate to a power of 2. So, confusingly to the uninitiated, a kilobyte (KB) actually has 1,024 bytes in it. With larger numbers this can lead to confusion. For example you get 16,384 characters in 16 KB; non-IT people tend to think, not unreasonably, that you should only get 16,000.

Megabyte

A million letters or numbers can be stored in a megabyte (MB). An A4 page of text will have about 500 words on it, needing roughly 5 to 10 KB to store it with a typical word processing package. So a megabyte would reasonably be expected to store up to 200 such pages. In reality word processing applications store all sorts of formatting, layout and application information and use much more space than this. This chapter used up 61,000 bytes but is only 1,500 words (8,000 characters) long: eight times as much memory as you might expect.

NOTE

Word processing packages have very non-linear storage requirements. For example the one used to write this book uses up a whole 19 KB to store a document whose sole content is the letter 'a'. However, it used 64 KB to store 3,000 words of material. Sizing is very dependent on what you store and what you store it with.

Megabytes are often the units used to measure working memory (known as RAM); a PC built in 2007 will normally have between 256 and 2,048 MB of this. The gigabyte (1,024 MB) is starting to be used here too.

Gigabyte

The gigabyte (GB) is the unit used to measure disk and memory size. Today PCs already routinely have 0.5 to 1 GB of RAM.

Terabyte

The terabyte (TB) is starting to take over from the gigabyte as the unit used for disk memory. A terabyte is 1,024 GB; at the time of writing PCs routinely came with 250 GB drives and 500 GB are not that rare. In fact you could currently buy a 1 TB standalone drive for under £100. So expect to see this in specifications, although unless you are storing large amounts of graphics/video you are unlikely to need this much for running your business.

> **NOTE**
>
> With large amounts of data it is important to be able to back it up to another media. For small systems it is often easiest to do this to DVDs. However, online storage via high-bandwidth broadband connections is becoming a viable and cost-effective alternative for both backup and for applications data. This is part of what is increasingly known as SaaS.

Petabyte

A petabyte (PB) is 1,024 TB. For an SME a petabyte is a lot of memory: if you are told you need it, ask why. In order to give this book a longer life, it is worth noting that the next step up from this is an exabyte (1,024 PB).

Solid state memory device

This is an alternative to a disk for 'hard' storage. These are widgets such as memory sticks and the memory cards that go in cameras etc.

RAM

The working memory of a computer measured in megabytes (or increasingly gigabytes); usually the more you have the better.

Bandwidth

How much information you can get from one place to another in a given time measured in kilobits to megabits per second. For example broadband download connection speeds currently range from about 1 to 8 Mb s^{-1} (although more and less is available). This means that a 1 Mb document should be with you in 8 to 10 seconds.

> **NOTE**
>
> With broadband connections a secondary feature is what is termed the 'contention ratio'. This represents how many people are sharing this bandwidth with you. As people do not use their connection to download all of the time, the suppliers do not provide a dedicated
> *(Continued)*

(Continued)

connection: they reduce costs by sharing the non-used time between several users; a dedicated line with the same performance would be very expensive. Contention ratios vary between 10:1 and 100:1. A contention ration of 50:1 is quite common for personal use: if all 50 of these users were to choose to download at the same time then your download speed would be 1/50 of the maximum speed; this is one reason why you experience variable performance with broadband services. If you are a business with multiple users, you might want to choose a connection with a lower contention ratio, but it will cost you more. You need to take into account both the speed and contention ratio when comparing different broadband offerings (and also the volume of data they allow you to move up and down the line per month: some are unlimited, others charge extra above a certain amount; nobody said it was simple). In addition you need to see if there are any 'volume' charges associated with your broadband connection. Some apparently 'good value' internet service providers (ISPs) charge for the volume of data as well as the connection, a bit like budget airlines who have cheap seat prices but charge a fortune if you have any luggage to put in the hold.

Disk

The hard disk drive (HDD) provides 'hard' storage space or memory. They come in various sizes (see gigabytes above and so forth). This gets cheaper, faster and larger as time passes. The more the better, although you need to be able to back it up for security. See the note following terabytes above.

Duty cycle

The duty cycle describes the number of operations a device should be able to perform in a time period. It is normally related to printers, used to describe how many pages per month they are designed to deliver (e.g. 5,000 pages per month). Small laser printers tend to have duty cycles around a few tens of thousands of pages per month. Small inkjets can have duty cycles as low as 1,000 pages per month. This needs to be appropriate for your actual use if reliability is required.

Graphics card and memory

This is a device that drives the visual display unit (hence the old term VDU) that you view images on. It can also be used to drive devices such as projectors and touch screen displays. The larger or higher the resolution the more expensive it will be. The same applies to the refresh rate it can support (the higher the rate the less potential for 'flicker' on the display). The larger the internal memory it has the higher the performance is likely to be. There are two standard connectors in use: the older 'VGA' (video graphics array) type connection for 'analogue' monitors and the newer 'DVI' (digital visual interface).

LAN

LAN denotes local area network, used to connect a number of PCs together at one, usually small, location. For an SME this is likely to be a few PCs in an office, maybe with a link to a workshop or store.

WAN

WAN denotes wide area network, used to connect you to the 'wider' world. A broadband connection to an ISP is the most common example that an SME will come across. As with all communications you will pay more for greater capacity (e.g. higher bandwidth).

Printer resolution

This is measured in dots per inch (dpi) vertically and horizontally and is essentially how sharp a picture you get when you print out your documents. The greater the number of dots, the better the result. As a minimum you might look for 300 dpi (for most documents 300 dpi is fine), but 600 dpi is commonplace now and higher resolutions are available at a reasonable cost.

Screen resolution

This is measured in pixels, the number of dots horizontally and vertically. As with printers the higher the resolution the better and price will be related to this. In practice for ordinary word processing you will be OK with 800 × 600, but most screens and graphic adapters will support at least 1,024 × 768 and 1,280 × 1,024 is common, although for the higher resolutions you will need to consider a larger screen (or spectacles). You will pay more for the larger screens, but if you are doing serious graphics or want many 'windows' open at the same then it is worth it.

Central processor speed

This is measured in gigahertz (GHz): the faster the better (higher value in gigahertz), although there is no point in paying for performance you do not need.

Graphics processor speed

The graphics processor speed is measured in megahertz (MHz): again the faster the better (higher value in megahertz), but do not pay for what you do not need. See also 'Graphics cards and memory' above.

Compact disc (CD)

Originally used for audio recordings in digital form, they have been widely adopted for PC application distribution and data backup (on read–write drives). They have a capacity of about 650 MB. A CD drive is a minimum expectation on a current PC. They have replaced the floppy disk.

Digital versatile disc (DVD)

Using different technology to the CD, but physically similar looking media, DVDs are both faster and capable of storing more data (typically 4.7 GB).

> **NOTE**
>
> As this book was being written two different technologies were battling it out for dominance as the next step along from DVDs. Sony's Blu-ray Disc and HD-DVD. Both deliver storage in the 20–50 GB area. There are drives that deal with both media and when a clear winner emerges these dual drives should be a consideration. They are currently expensive but will reduce in price soon, as everything in IT does.

The World Wide Web (WWW)

Invented by Sir Tim Berners-Lee this is the face of the internet that most of us see. It is where the retail sites, IT manufacturers, special interest groups, societies, academic institutions, your business and so on have their public face on the internet.

Client–server

A client–server architecture involves keeping data and applications on a central computer (server) supporting users on some form of PC (clients). This has been the mainstream solution for most large and medium sized businesses for many years. You have a central machine with significant amounts of memory and storage that has the applications and user data kept on it. This has the benefit of providing a central place for backing up and supporting disaster recovery and so forth. Users access it from their PCs via some form of LAN or in some cases LAN+WAN.

SPEED OF CHANGE

Moore's law springs to mind again here. Gordon Moore, co-founder of the Intel Corporation, forecast that the number of transistors on a microprocessor would double approximately every 18 months. In real terms this implies the that price performance of IT equipment doubles in a similar period (there are similar laws for disk capacity price performance). This forecast was made in the 1970s and if anything has proved to be pessimistic: in 2007 it is actually increasing.

KEY POINT

As long as the IT you have does what you need then do not feel obliged to keep up with the change. As long as it does the job and you can still get support for it when you need to, then you are OK.

CONSUMABLE VERSUS CAPITAL ITEMS

In the 1980s everything associated with the computer industry was very, very expensive. Even a keyboard was an item that demanded an asset tag; the computers themselves were high-ticket items. In 2007 much of IT comes into the disposable category: you can buy an entire PC, with operating system, mouse, keyboard and flat screen display for not much over £300 (€420 at the exchange rate at the time of writing) and that is at retail, one-off volumes.

Consequently it has become hard to determine what you treat as capital equipment and what you treat as a consumable. Indeed consumables, for example inkjet and laser cartridges for printers, can cost far more per year than the capital cost of the printers themselves.

MAINTENANCE

The extent to which maintenance matters can vary significantly within the SME sector: some need nothing at all; others need a full-blown, all-inclusive, outsourced maintenance service.

EXAMPLE 1

The author has absolutely no maintenance support in place (other than any warranty that comes with new equipment). This has never been a problem in nearly 20 years as the author is IT literate and all of the equipment is sufficiently cheap to be treated as essentially disposable. There are sufficient PCs available to ensure that should one fail there is always one available to carry on any urgent work, you can always buy a new PC within hours and so forth. Critical to the success of this strategy is having accessible backups of data and applications or OS and sufficient IT knowledge to install and reconfigure as needed. In fact the costs of even the simplest maintenance support for the installed equipment would be unjustifiable here.

EXAMPLE 2

The example here is a market research company (12 people) with no in-depth IT knowledge, a small network (wired and wireless) with a server and networked printers. They have enough personal knowledge to do minor jobs such as installing a PC or office suite and the like but not to fix problems or configure networks and servers. Consequently they chose to outsource the operation, disaster recovery and maintenance of their server and the support of their network. Key to this arrangement was defining boundaries for responsibilities and service levels needed to support the business. The cost of the service is not trivial, but the option of 'popping out to the shops when something breaks' is not realistic and this is an unavoidable business overhead. However, not having to spend valuable fee earning time on IT and having peace of mind that the IT is there to support the delivery of their services makes this a benefit rather than a burden.

In addition qualified and experienced IT staff can be expensive, as can their training. Outsourcing enables clients to focus on their core capability whilst gaining access to the latest technologies and qualified staff. Training costs to keep ahead of the game are incurred by the outsourcer.

EXAMPLE 3

This example is a recruitment company with over 200 people. Here the organisation is large enough to have its own albeit small IT department and has different strategies for different areas of IT. In the case of desktop PCs they have no maintenance support: they have a couple of preconfigured spares (and people can always use the PC of someone off sick or on holiday in an emergency). The policy is to throw it away when it breaks (beyond the ability of the in-house staff to fix it economically) and get a new one. They unbundle (i.e. get a price reduction for not having any) warranty where they can, rather than bothering with getting faults fixed by suppliers. They maintain their own networks (wired and wireless).

In all of these examples the key to maintenance provision is matching the supply to the needs of the business. It should not be driven by whatever IT equipment is there, but by what is needed to support the delivery of the business services or products to the clients. Otherwise there is a risk of over investment leading to a poor return on investment. The key is to have the right tool for the job. As with all IT procurements you should look at maintenance in terms of a business case rather than just cost.

It is worth noting at this point that the maintenance provision chosen will make up a significant part of the TCO of any IT equipment or service.

In fact for PC-type equipment the TCO may be largely made up of the maintenance and support element and the capital cost can be insignificant. Table 8.1 lists points to consider when looking at maintenance supply. See also the notes on SLAs in Chapter 11.

TABLE 8.1   *Points to consider when looking at maintenance supply*

Consideration	Measurements	Notes
Availability	Percentage	Defines the availability of the service within agreed service hours. Can be very expensive. When high figures are specified, e.g. more than 98% (where there is no resilience built into the infrastructure), the time available to fix is very limited. If higher figures are required, then additional investment in failover or standby equipment is needed. It is vital that availability requirements are driven by actual, real business needs, otherwise the return on investment is poor.
Time to respond	Hours or days, percentage	Simply how long before they respond to your call. This can cover everything from the time to answer an initial phone call or email through to the time before an engineer visits your site (if needed). The initial response should be a few rings for a phone call and within a few minutes to an hour for an email (depending on priority; see the 'Priority or urgency' entry).
Time to fix	Hours or days, percentage	This will be driven by the priority assigned to each incident or problem.
Hours of service	Range of hours or days	At the top level you get the proverbial 24/7: all day every day all year. This is always going to have an associated cost.
SLA	Various	Part of the contractual agreement between the supplier and the client that details what services are to be supplied and what measurements apply to them. Can be expected to cover all of the items in this table and more. It is essential that you understand what it implies: 'What you measure is what you get.'
Priority or urgency	Number, e.g. 1 highest, 3 lowest	Specifies how urgent a problem is (a good point here is who determines this). Priority is usually driven by a combination of the impact to the business and the urgency to get it fixed. Some organisations have a VIP list: these people automatically receive priority attention. Some organisations have developed quite complex priority coding systems. If your SME needs such a system then get the supplier to explain why and how it will work.
Escalation	Time	There should be an escalation process that says what happens when faults do not get fixed or are not fixed within agreed times.

(Continued)

TABLE 8.1   *(Continued)*

Consideration	Measurements	Notes
Penalties or service credits	Money	This is something that is found in the SLAs for very large organisations, but the author is not aware of how it has been made to work in SMEs other than at a very simple level of a refund for missed calls above a specified level. It is worth noting that in large organisations such arrangements often have a risk/reward element where over-performance is rewarded to encourage service improvement.

A major element of any maintenance contract will be a SLA. This will (should) cover all aspects of the maintenance service you receive and can include penalty clauses or service credits that determine what happens when the supplier fails to deliver as per the agreement. It may even include rewards for exceeding the basic service. All of this requires careful study and negotiation to ensure that the SLA you have is appropriate for your business.

SLAs are organic agreements and should evolve to reflect the changing business. Given that research suggests that SMEs over 10 people in size have ambitious growth targets, they are likely to have continual change. At the very least, a full review of the SLA should be undertaken annually and this should be a collaborative exercise between the customer and supplier. SLA targets must also be achievable, measurable and clearly defined. Suppliers will often want a baselining period at the start of the partnership in order to assess that the infrastructure they are taking on is able to deliver against SLA targets. Targets can then be negotiated up or down accordingly as the business evolves.

KEY POINT

Keep in mind that what you measure is what you get and you need to make sure that the contract or SLA is appropriate for your business. If it is not then you may find you incur additional charges to get what you want or that your business cannot function properly (e.g. if you have to wait too long to get a vital system back online after a fault).

LEGACY ISSUES

As a company grows from a handful of staff to tens and twenties, it is likely to go through significant change in the IT in use. It might start out with a couple of PCs that belonged to the company's founders (in one case a PC was actually purloined from the teenage son of the founder). These could easily have old versions of applications software.

CASE STUDY

Chapter House Training (the wife of the author's business) specialises in all forms of communications training such as presentations, public speaking and working in teams. It has been in business for nearly 20 years and has been using IT to support the business since the beginning. The very first computer, an IBM PS2 with an HP laser printer, was obtained in exchange for a training course. This ran an early version of Windows and had an early copy of Adobe PageMaker. It was used to produce course material such as handouts and course notes. After 14 years the PS2 and the printer were still in use, sitting on a network as a printer server. Also on the network by this time were a laptop and a newer PC, a 'clone'. These were running Windows 95 and 98; PageMaker was in use, in parallel with Word from Microsoft's Office Suite. At the time of writing the PS2 has now been retired (it still worked but had run out of upgrade ability and was not able to support a newer printer when the original finally died; in any case with 5 MB of RAM and a 40 MB disk it was not up to modern needs). However, the Windows 95 machine is still in use, acting as a printer–scanner server, as is the Windows 98 laptop. The newest and only operating system still in support is Windows 2000. Newer versions of Word are in use and PageMaker is still used to update old material. Very little has been wasted and the return on investment has been immense. Of course this would not be supportable in a large organisation and has been dependent on the author's IT know-how to keep it all going. It currently has a broadband connection, modern email and an office suite that is compatible with that of mainstream conglomerates. The key point here is that an SME can be very flexible and gain real savings by being able to tolerate and recycle IT equipment and software that a large-scale operation could not. It also says much for the oft-criticised Microsoft that these disparate machines continue to talk to each other. Indeed there is nothing stopping these systems being linked to wireless networks and remote devices including Blackberrys and other personal digital assistant (PDA) related devices.

COMPLEXITY

What makes IT projects difficult and notoriously prone to disaster is their potential for complexity. For the small and micro end of the SME market this is less likely to be an issue.

ALTERNATIVE STRATEGIES (INCLUDING SaaS)

Although this section is mainly aimed at the 'S' end of the market, where money is always tightest, it contains food for thought for anyone buying IT that wants to cut costs. It is actually possible to cut IT costs dramatically if you can step outside the mainstream. By the mainstream we mean the big name suppliers such as Microsoft, Apple, Oracle and so forth.

Sources

For software the jargon words here are: freeware, shareware and openware. These all lead to lower costs than the more conventional sources.

Freeware

Freeware is copyrighted computer software which is made available for use free of charge, for an unlimited time. Authors of freeware often want to 'give something to the community', but also want credit for their software and to retain control of its future development. This has been around a very long time: go into any newsagents and look at the home computing magazines and there usually will be at least one with a 'bumper' freeware CD or DVD attached.

> **KEY POINT**
>
> Always consider risk versus (lower) price when selecting freeware for anything that is critical to your business. Can you afford to have it break down? Also be very, very careful when installing anything whose origins you are not sure of: always check for computer viruses.

Shareware

The same disks that carry freeware often have even more shareware. The difference is that shareware is not free. Charging may be based on try before you buy with a time limit, upgrades to useable versions or donations to charity, but invariably it requires a fee to be legal. One of the best-known shareware applications is the file compression program WinZip. (www.winzip.com/)

Openware

Very much community based, there is a significant body of openware available for use. This software is typically supported and distributed by a community of highly skilled technologists.

Perhaps the best-known example is distributed by Sun Microsystems and is called OpenOffice. This is a complete office suite offering word processing, presentation software, spreadsheet, database, a mathematical equation tool and a drawing package. It started out in life as StarOffice but now has the backing of a major manufacturer, although support is provided by the user community. This support comes both for free and also commercially. There is also training, training literature and documentation, and a host of specialist add-ons. It can also generate files that are compatible with commercial office suites such as Microsoft Office™. It represents a low-risk option for the SME and is available as a download for free or for a few tens of pounds as a CD or DVD. (www.openoffice.org/)

> **KEY POINT**
>
> Decide whether you need to be compatible with the mainstream because your clients insist on it.

Advantages

Taking the path less trodden has one major advantage: cost. You will be able to obtain most of the basic software you need for a minimal cost.

Risks

There is an old saying in the IT industry: 'No one got fired for buying IBM.' In other words if you choose from the mainstream it is hard for anyone to say you made a bad decision: it is the safe choice.

There are risks associated with the alternative sources for software or hardware. These come in three categories: compatibility, skills and support. Table 8.2 gives some examples to consider when looking at an alternate approach. Use these as a starting point when analysing your own situation.

TABLE 8.2   *Points to consider when looking at an alternative approach*

Compatibility	Skills	Support
If you have to deal with mainstream corporate organisations then they are likely to be using standard office suites. You may need to be compatible with them to communicate and exchange documents effectively.	Using non-standard applications can make getting hold of staff who can use them more difficult.	If you are not technically adept then support will matter to you. Some freeware and shareware applications are very much 'as is' and if you rely on them you could get into difficulties.
A large amount of information that is available via the internet or from suppliers tends to be in a format that is compatible with the standard office suites. However, if you choose an application that cannot import or export this then you may be isolated.	Training for non-standard applications may be harder to come by.	Open-source software still leaves you with a non-contractual support system, although you can often pay for this if you prefer.

(Continued)

TABLE 8.2 *(Continued)*

Compatibility	Skills	Support
Third-party applications may not communicate effectively with such products. Also, where the platform suppliers (e.g. of the hardware or operating system software) make changes there may be no guarantee that your applications continue to run unchanged.	People straight from school, college or university are more likely to have had experience on mainstream applications.	If your support structure is insufficient to keep your systems running as needed, then it may impact your business and make any savings a false economy.

NOTE

See also the SaaS section below for some risks to consider associated with security and access to data.

Online applications (including SaaS)

Online applications are relatively new to the market. One of the pioneers of this, at the time of writing, is Google who launched Google Apps™ Premier Edition at the end of February 2007. This supplies a basic online office suite that costs a few tens of pounds per year per user. It includes access to email, instant messaging, a calendar system, word processing and spreadsheets. This compares very favourably with traditional suppliers of such software who charge hundreds of pounds per copy and usually produce a new version every few years for a reduced but significant upgrade fee.

In an interview with *Computer Weekly* at the time of the Google Apps™ launch, the director of information at the UK Highways Agency Denise Plumpton said that:

> It is clearly aiming to position itself as a major player in the market, and I think it stands a good chance of eroding Microsoft's customer base.

It is very likely that the supply of online applications will be a growth market, particularly for SMEs who can save not only capital costs but also support costs. Google will have competitors and that can only make prices even lower.

SaaS

As mentioned above this is relatively new, but follows a trend based on ever-increasing economies of scale for storage and processing provision that is also showing up in the online media provision. This is evidenced by the decline in music CD sales in the face of competition from online sources. This trend is starting to be seen in video too: investment in a DVD recording system may be premature.

In some ways it is like a step back in IT history: in the early days companies had large centralised mainframe computers that people accessed via 'dumb' terminals. Now we have vast distributed storage and processing which we access over the internet with PCs essentially acting as display and input devices.

The main risks and benefits of SaaS are listed in Table 8.3. Two common examples of SaaS applications include Google Apps™ and Citrix™ (there are links to these in the list of useful websites at the end of the book).

TABLE 8.3   *The main risks and benefits of SaaS*

Risks	Benefits
• Lack of control: you are at the mercy of the supplier; should they wish to change the applications you may have no choice but to follow with any retraining/changes to operating practices that may be needed. • Security: you are dependent on the supplier having appropriate safeguards in place to keep your data confidential. • Continuity: you are dependent on them having good backup and disaster recovery procedures in place to protect your service provision. • Cannot access if your network, ISP or broadband connection fails: this will potentially stop all your access and shut you down until the fault is found and fixed.	• As it is likely to be 'Web 2.0' based it can be accessed from a low-spec PC using a standard browser (e.g. Internet Explorer, Godzilla etc.). • Can be pay as you go controlling costs on the basis of paying only for what you use. • Reduces administration and operational overhead: you do not have to backup data, operate servers and look after licences etc. • Data security and disaster recovery should be done for you, saving cost and headaches. • You have access to the latest applications and/or cheap applications as you choose.

KEY POINT

SaaS is likely to be a major growth area and no SME can afford not to consider it. It is particularly attractive to a start-up, providing that you can get training or staff who can use the applications and you are happy that the risks are controlled.

Hardware

For hardware, the jargon words are plug compatible. This term originally came from the mainframe world when computers filled up huge rooms and there were only a few manufacturers. New entrants to the IT market created their own 'plug compatible products'. The internals were their own but to all intents and purposes they behaved in the same way as the original. They were usually cheaper, faster or had more capacity than the big name product. This is most apparent with the PC: the impact of competition is such that there is no great difference between the big name supplier and the unknown and such that the price difference is not that great between the two. In fact the price of PCs and related equipment is so low that few will need to shop around for a deal here.

However, a lower specification or last year's model can bring savings that are perhaps important to some.

Operating systems and core components

This comes into one of two categories: proprietary systems from the mainstream suppliers and open-source systems from a variety of sources. Microsoft has the majority market in the proprietary PC-based systems with their Windows™ range and has the monopoly on its source. Linux-based open systems are well known and well developed across a range of hardware.

Applications software

This is where the real savings are available for the SME. There is nothing wrong with buying a brand name, market-dominating applications such as Microsoft's Office Suite. In fact much of this book was written using it. However, you do not have to; for example OpenOffice (www.openoffice.org/) is available as a free download and provides a feature-rich office suite that includes word processing, spreadsheets, drawing tools, database and desktop publishing applications. These applications are compatible with common 'brand' applications. What is more, with some backing from Sun Microsystems and having its own 'community' based support organisation this is a low-risk option. For the smaller organisation that needs basic productivity tools and does not require complex product integration and technical support this can be a real money saver.

CASE STUDY

The author has a modest need for graphics applications for diagrams and the like. Rather than invest in applications that are feature rich (with features that will not be used), the author uses shareware and freeware packages. These produce illustrations in standard formats (e.g. JPEG and TIFF files) that are compatible with all mainstream applications. As the sole user the skills issues do not apply; a larger organisation might not be able to adopt such a strategy.

KEY POINT

You can get the tools to do the job for surprisingly low prices, even for free, if you are prepared to do some research and/or consider alternative sources.

TRAINING

This is a much-neglected topic; many SMEs buy systems and services and then find that they do not actually have the ability to use them effectively. The three most common approaches to training are teach yourself, in-house training and external courses. Table 8.4 covers the pros and cons of these from an SME perspective.

TABLE 8.4 *Pros and cons of the most common approaches to training*

Method	Notes	Pros	Cons
Teach yourself	This can vary from sitting down at the keyboard and embarking on a trial and error process, through reading the manual or textbook, to computer-based training (CBT).	Cost, at least capital cost. Can be fitted in with other activities so creating less disruption.	Can take longer, so slower to become productive. May not learn 'best practice' and so be less effective.
In-house training	A larger (i.e. an 'M') may have an actual training department or in-house trainers; a smaller organisation may depend on 'sitting with Nellie', a more experienced user.	Convenience, easily tailored to your needs, flexibility in timing and location.	May not be practical to cover all applications in use. Quality of 'lead user' training may not be as high as a professional trainer.
External courses	Either off-the-shelf or bespoke courses either delivered onsite or at a training centre, hotel etc.	Should be of a high standard and cover 'best practice', although this is by no means guaranteed (obtain references).	Can be expensive, if not bespoke then may not be ideal for your needs.

KEY POINT

If you do not train your staff or yourself to the standard you need to run your business effectively then you will have problems. An investment

(Continued)

(Continued)

in IT and productivity systems is completely wasted if people cannot use it. The author was involved in implementing a post-installation training programme for a major supermarket that had installed a new stock management system. The system was failing to deliver, including damaging customer experience from lack of produce on the shelves, because staff could not understand how it worked. It was an expensive training exercise to overcome something that should never have been a problem.

OUTSOURCING

When this book was commissioned the author made it clear that outsourcing was out of the scope. The subject is very complex and would justify a whole book in its own right (some examples are provided in the reference list). Also it is more appropriate for those with large IT functions to outsource in the first place, not the target audience for this book. Most SMEs do not have a large enough IT function for it to be worth outsourcing the whole thing. However, many SMEs do outsource business functions such as accounting and PAYE. Similarly IT maintenance is often passed on to a third-party supplier. Also the development of online applications, such as Google Apps™, is a form of outsourcing. So this section has crept into the book to provide the briefest of notes on the subject; no apology is made for its brevity, this book is really for the novice and outsourcing is a complex option not to be entered into without expert knowledge to hand.

Outsourcing or subcontracting?

It can be argued that 'focused' outsourcing, where you just outsource a particular element, is just another from of subcontracting. This is a good point, perhaps the differentiator is that when you outsource something you leave all aspects of the service provision to them: you do not specify how they do it, just the outcome.

Pros

The idea is that by outsourcing elements (or all) of your IT to a specialist third party you benefit from their expertise and economies of scale.

Cons

The negatives come from loss of control and not having your IT run to fit your business, possible inflexibility when you want to change and having to make your internal IT compatible with the platforms that the outsource company uses.

Points to consider

The first point to consider is, what is in it for me? You need to have a real, measurable benefit or it is not worth considering. Usually this will be cost related, but it may be that you can obtain a better level of service than you can afford internally (e.g. 24/7 support for your servers). The most important consideration is that it is measurable and enforceable: if they do not meet the target you should be compensated (see also SLAs as in Chapter 11 and elsewhere).

The next point to consider is that an outsource provider is no different to any other supplier. You must evaluate them against the criteria that you would apply to any supplier such as track record, financial stability and so forth.

KEY POINT

Do not outsource anything critical to your business that you are not happy to lose control of.

Easier outsourcing options

There are some elements of IT that any SME can consider outsourcing without losing control or flexibility. They are listed in Table 8.5 together with some brief notes; they can be taken individually or in combination. They are all elements that can be procured within the scope of the procurement practices described in this book. The author has found SMEs that subcontract or outsource; the choice of words is left to the reader.

TABLE 8.5 *Easier IT service outsourcing options*

IT service	Comments
Maintenance	In particular hardware maintenance. Unless you can afford to employ or are lucky enough to have someone with the basic knowledge to deal with day-to-day faults then you need this service. There are a wide range of local and national service providers to choose from. At the subcontract level this would be along the lines of a call-out to fix a fault (break fix support). However, at the outsource level, particularly when combined with applications software support, this could be a complete helpdesk and pre-emptive maintenance service.
Applications provision	As described in the section on SaaS there are one-stop shops that will provide your applications, data storage and backup etc. all available online.
Long-term storage and backup	Can be done over broadband services via ISPs and the like or can be subcontracted to people who will run your server systems for you.
Server hosting	For an SME this can be very effective and attractive. The hosting supplier sells you a package that includes how much data you can store, processing capacity, availability of service, security (for both backups and access to data), continuity and so forth. It can be difficult to replicate this in house at a reasonable cost.

(Continued)

TABLE 8.5   *(Continued)*

IT service	Comments
ISP services	Unless you operate as an ISP yourself then you will need to get this from elsewhere. There is a wide range of suppliers to choose from.
Training	Widely available both as self-taught, distance learning and classroom (onsite as well as offsite). Research is helpful when choosing what is best for you.
Disaster recovery	You can get third parties to provide business continuity services such as backup servers, preconfigured PCs and the like. This is something that is entirely a financial decision of cost versus impact. For an SME, providing you have backups you can use, it can often be cheaper to have a disaster recovery strategy based on replacing a broken PC.

SUMMARY

For the majority of SMEs the IT they employ will be mainstream. If they have specialist needs then they are likely to be specialists themselves with the appropriate level of knowledge. Owing to this they should be able to separate out what they actually want from the technology-specific elements. To a very large extent much IT is now a commodity item and it is not until you reach more complex, integrated systems that the purchaser will need more than basic knowledge. That basic knowledge is available relatively inexpensively from local specialists; these will often be cheaper than big organisations and are more likely to give a tailored service to the smaller client.

Organisations at the small end of the scale can more easily take advantage of alternative strategies and make potentially large savings. They must take into account any risks (for example ease of finding staff with appropriate skills) when doing this but it is a real opportunity.

Organisations at the larger end of the SME spectrum are likely to have more complex and difficult systems. In this case they need to consider the costs of an external specialist support organisation versus having their own internal specialists. This decision will have a significant impact on how they go about their procurements.

9 Suppliers

In this chapter we cover dealing with suppliers, issuing documents to them, meetings and briefings, questions, reference site visits, giving them feedback and being seen to be fair.

INTRODUCTION

Suppliers are a fact of life if you need to buy anything. They may be internal or external to your organisation (although for most SMEs they are likely to be external and that is the assumption here) but you will be their customer. The customer–supplier relationship is one that needs to be worked at for things to go well. For the complex, long-term procurements that are common in IT you need to be working towards a long-term partnership relationship where you are working to achieve a common goal. Your aim should be to choose suppliers who see your success as being their success.

Much of this chapter is aimed at the more complex purchase, but even if you are only buying a memory stick for £10 you will still find relevant material.

The last part of this chapter will cover some of the sales techniques that you might encounter: some of these may actually be helpful to you; some may not keep your best interests to the fore.

WHAT SUPPLIERS NEED

Having spent a significant amount of time on the bidders or suppliers side of the fence author has developed a marked sensitivity for poorly defined requirements and imprecise instructions to bidders. The more precise and clear you are the greater the chance of getting the response you want and the less effort you will need to reach a good decision.

So what suppliers need is a complete, unambiguous definition of what you want. Of course this is the real world; if you knew all of this then you would probably be an IT consultancy business yourself. Also what you learn from your suppliers may change what you want; things change and there is a degree of iteration in any significant procurement. In fact if your procurement takes more than a very short time you, your business, the suppliers and technology are likely to have changed anyway. Even if your procurement documentation was perfect when produced it will not remain so for long. Most suppliers know this, but aim for the ideal and it will give them the best chance of helping you. This also includes telling them about yourselves: they need enough information to be able to meet your specific needs.

Honesty and openness should be a given. If you mislead your supplier it can only end up in recriminations further down the line. There are those who say that you should never tell a supplier what your budget for work is, the argument being that if they know how much money you have then they will try and spend it, even if it is not what you need. The author's view is that if they do this, do not trade with them. However, if you are going to a number of suppliers then competition will keep them keen. Also, you only need to give a rough guide, you do not need to put it in writing; an informal chat will do during preliminary talks. In fact doing this early on in the process is a good idea. The benefit to you and the supplier is that unrealistic combinations of requirements and budget can be identified before either of you waste time. It can also help identify cheaper or more expensive options that might be better for you both.

EXAMPLE

A trivial but important example comes from a craft manufacturer SME who lacked trust in anything to do with IT. As they did not want to be ripped off they suggested to their suppliers that they had a very specific maximum budget (not actually true) and that no quote beyond this would be tolerated. They wanted a hosted service combined with a website to put the business in the ebusiness arena. They obtained only one quote, for the amount stated as a maximum and this reinforced their view that the suppliers were all grasping rogues; two other suppliers refused to quote on the grounds that you could not do a good job for the money and they were ill-advised to carry on. The SME ignored the common complaint from all of the suppliers: that they were not going to get a decent system for anything like the price they could afford and urging them to think again. They stuck to their guns and got what looked like the world's most basic website with a non-automated backend: to place an order you sent an email with your phone number and the SME then had to phone you back to process any credit card and payment details before manually producing an invoice etc. to dispatch with the goods. The site was not a success and further reinforced the beliefs of the SME who gave up on it feeling that the suppliers had not delivered. In fact for only about 50% more, a sum that was affordable, they could have a much slicker, user-friendly system that might have generated worthwhile business. A self-fulfilling prophecy: if the SME had been a little more open (even not actually specifying a maximum would have helped), then things could have been different.

KEY POINT

Give feedback: suppliers like to know how they are doing and why they won or lost. It is in your interest to do this as they can then do a better job for you next time.

WHAT TO EXPECT (OR DEMAND) OF A SUPPLIER

Approachable and open

One thing to keep in mind is that if a supplier does not treat you well before you buy from them then there is little chance they will treat you well afterwards. The level of service you get pre-sale is the benchmark for after-sales service. However, this still means you should be reasonable.

Honesty and openness should be the number one demand you make of a supplier. You cannot be honest and open with them if they are not honest and open with you and this mutual respect is important for the long-term relationship.

This applies equally to commodity and small purchases as it does to complex solution providers. They should give you accurate information about stock levels, lead times and prices. If they do not have your mouse in stock they should say so.

> **KEY POINT**
>
> If you do not think a supplier is being honest with you or if you simply do not like the way they do business then do not trade with them. Even if you are wrong, it will not work out unless you have a good working relationship.

Comprehensibility

IT can be a complex subject for the non-specialist. The supplier is the specialist (hopefully) and it is up to them to explain things so that you can understand them.

Support

One good measure of a supplier is the support they give you after they have made the sale. It is also a good indicator pre-sale. If they do not look after you before they have your money then they are unlikely to do so after they have been paid.

Legal responsibilities

Chapter 11 deals with legal issues in general and there is a plethora of legislation, both commercial and environmental, that can apply. You might want to note that under the Sale of Goods Act 1979 traders must sell goods that are as described and of satisfactory quality. Since 1 January 2007 they are also responsible under the WEEE Directive for financing the collection, treatment, recycling and recovery of WEEE. The Supply of Goods and Services Act 1982 requires traders to provide services to a proper standard of workmanship.

WHAT NOT TO EXPECT (OR DEMAND) OF A SUPPLIER

It works both ways: how you treat your supplier pre-sale is going to affect how they treat you too. Do not expect them to spend large amounts of time on you if there is no real intention to proceed. Do not use them for free consultancy and do not keep asking for endless quotes if you are not genuinely going to buy. Losing business to a rival on price, delivery or service is part of the game, but being messed around is not.

Do not ask for too many favours until you have established a working relationship. Yes you are the customer and so should be treated as a 'king', but like all relationships it has to be built up over time and be even-handed.

Do not expect them to be able to meet stupid deadlines; check with them first before making demands. It is not clever or reasonable to make them work through a weekend to turn round your request for a proposal because you were late asking for it.

Do not ask for interest-free credit because you did not pay their invoices on time.

Do not expect or accept rudeness from them under any circumstances. If a supplier's representative or employee does not treat you courteously then escalate the matter to their boss if you do not get an apology fairly quickly. People have bad days and the odd slip is reasonable, but you deserve politeness even if you are at fault.

Do not expect them to have an in-depth knowledge of your organisation. It is reasonable to expect them to know something about the industries they sell to, but it is up to you to fill them in on your own world.

CUSTOMER–SUPPLIER RELATIONSHIPS

If you have read through what to expect and not to expect then you will have got the gist of this already. The key word is relationship. It pays to establish long-term relationships that are mutually beneficial with any supplier. That way, when you have a genuine urgent need then you are more likely to be accommodated.

However, if all does not go well it is helpful to have some grounding in conflict handling and resolution. This can be looked on as a special case of negotiation and Chapter 10 has useful information that will help. Here we offer a potted conflict-handling checklist that can be used to resolve issues.

Overview of conflict handling

Introduction

Life is difficult, but like growing old it is better than the alternative. In particular working life can be fraught with difficulties; these come in many forms but are usually caused by your colleagues, customers and suppliers. There is no way to avoid these troubles and tribulations but there are things you can do to make them easier to deal with. This conflict handling section will show you how to use communication skills to make dealing with difficult situations easier. It also shows how poor communication is often at the root of many conflicts.

Causes

Practical research has shown that there are five main causes of conflict as follows:

(i) Assumptions: you cannot be sure that everyone has the same assumptions until they are tested.

(ii) Communication: when this is poor you can be working with incomplete information.

(iii) Priority: individuals have different priorities regarding people and tasks.

(iv) Speed: people have different speeds and ways of working.

(v) Status or territory: this concerns space, money, power or even a desire to keep secrets.

KEY POINT

The reader should note the difference between assertion and aggression. Aggression is based on contempt for others; people who act this way are relying on others to cave in. Assertiveness is based on respect for both yourself and for those with whom you deal. Successful assertive behaviour includes being able to communicate what you feel clearly and being able to say what you want whilst taking into account how this will affect others.

Good conflict handling

The essence of good conflict handling is taking a step back, finding the facts, looking at the situation from as many angles as possible, asking people to explain what they think should happen, looking for the best possible situation all round and selling its benefits to all concerned.

When conflict arises there are several strategies for handling it. These can be divided into three types: aggressive, passive and assertive:

- **Aggressive:** 'I win, you lose'; dismiss the opposition.
- **Passive:** put it off; compromise.
- **Assertive:** look at both sides; find a solution.

Aggressive strategies

These strategies use no negotiation. They are not concerned with the possible merit or justice of the other party's case, simply with winning the conflict. These strategies invariably result in a win–lose situation which may be very well for the victor, but is no good for the vanquished. Conflicts that are managed in this way are not really resolved: they usually recur later when the vanquished has regrouped, restored their strength and have the (probably quite legitimate) feeling that they are 'owed' something.

There are some times in business when there can be no negotiation, for instance over things such as safety procedures, legal procedures or breach of contract. However, the attitude 'I will win at all costs' is not the most effective; it is far better to use one of the assertive strategies instead. In the case of a business negotiation (for instance over the cost of a product or service), the 'I win, you lose' strategy is in the main rather silly; it is not really worth gaining an individual sale if you eventually lose a supplier you might need in the future.

Passive strategies

These strategies result in a lose–lose situation, where neither party gets the result they wanted. The conflict is never really resolved and will recur later. There is, however, some merit in the 'put it off' strategy when tempers are running high and a period of 'cooling off' would make the next stage of the conflict management easier.

Assertive strategies

These are the most successful strategies, resulting in a win–win situation and a true resolution of the conflict. Be prepared to spend extra time when using these strategies since they involve a thorough investigation of both sides of the argument and careful planning of the outcome of the conflict. The following section gives some advice on how to achieve 'best practice'.

Conflict management 'best practice'

Define the problem

First you need a clear statement of what is going wrong, what has caused the conflict and how each person feels about this. Until the problem has been carefully defined, neither party can be certain of what is actually happening. There is a natural tendency in all of us to see our side of things clearly and pay much less attention to the other side's viewpoints.

At this point each person involved in the conflict should clearly state what has been happening. An effort must be made to hear the other person out calmly and there should be no interruptions (a neutral mediator or facilitator is extremely useful at this point).

RULES

- No interrupting.
- Talk about what has actually occurred, not what you think should have happened.

(Continued)

(Continued)
- No personal attacks or 'name calling'.
- Calmly ask for clarification if any of the points made are unclear.
- No general statements; be as precise as possible.
- All sides must put their case.
- Summarise at the end of each statement.

Analyse the causes

What caused the problem? Again all sides must contribute; a genuine attempt to understand why the problem or conflict has arisen and a genuine desire to resolve the conflict must be present.

RULES

- No interrupting.
- Try to keep to the subject: extraneous matter should not be dragged in.
- Try not to use 'blaming' language: you are not looking at whose fault it is, just at what started the conflict.
- All sides must put their case.
- Summarise at the end of each statement.

Look for a solution

Each party should try to define what they would like as an outcome of the conflict. This should not be a listing of reparations or demands, but a careful statement of what they would like to occur in terms of actions.

RULES

- No interrupting.
- Look for positive outcomes.
- Any solutions should be reasonable and must look at what limits and restrictions exist.
- Try to be creative.

Select a solution

Most conflicts within the business arena are solvable; we are not talking about hostage taking or the War on Terror. A reasonable solution is always possible if both parties genuinely want the conflict to cease. It is probable that most of the demands made at the height of the conflict were exaggerated or simply a bargaining position that can be adjusted later. By now, if the first three stages have been covered, it will be much easier for the parties to talk more reasonably and see that a positive outcome is possible. It is at this stage that the 'trade-off' principle comes into force: 'If you do such and such, then I'll do this and that' is a good starting point.

RULES

- Keep the idea that a solution is possible to the fore.
- You are not making concessions; you are trying to solve the problem.
- Think of the consequences if the conflict is not resolved.
- Be fair.

Implement the solution

Make an action plan. What will need to be done to stop the conflict reoccurring? Make a real commitment to communicate throughout the resolution of the conflict. Feedback is essential; just because you have decided what you are going to do does not mean that each person involved believes that this will happen. If the conflict was severe and the solution is complicated it may be necessary to put in some controls such as deadlines for remedial action or procedures that will ensure that changes really take place.

RULES

- No 'dragging the body about' or recriminations.
- Be positive.
- Use realistic timescales.
- Keep a record of what you have agreed to do.
- Both sides must agree.

SUPPLIER MEETINGS

It is inevitable that you will have to spend time with your suppliers to establish both a working relationship and a common understanding of what you need. This means meetings. Some notes are offered here to help you through the most common types of meetings you will have with potential suppliers.

Briefing suppliers

Make sure that you have all of the information you need to hand before the briefing and that you are all happy with it. Have people available who have sufficient knowledge to answer questions that the suppliers may have. For example if legacy systems are involved then have someone who understands them on hand; if implementing a network then you may need to have someone who knows about the building and so forth.

Ensure that the room you use is large enough to accommodate all those who need to attend and has any aids, such as projectors, screens, flip charts etc. that may be needed. Do not forget tea and coffee and car parking and transport issues.

KEY POINT

Be brief and clear but encourage them to ask questions and demonstrate to you that they have understood what you have presented.

Supplier presentations to you

Very much as per briefing suppliers; if they do not say what they will need, how many people are attending and so on then ask.

KEY POINT

Ask questions and if there is anything you do not understand ask for an explanation. If there is no time, ask them to arrange a further meeting; if they cannot explain it to you then consider another supplier.

Informal and formal meetings

For complex (and even some relatively simple) procurements there will always be meetings. These will cover things such as business plans, definition of requirements, progress meetings, bid approval, proposal and supplier reviews, analysis of supplier documents, pricing and so forth. A considerable amount of time will be spent in arranging and helping with such meetings. This can be wasted when meetings descend into talking shops where the original point of the meeting is forgotten because there was no agenda or one of the key people was missing.

The administrative tasks include the following:

- **Location and facilities**. Make sure the room is booked; block book in advance for regular meetings such as weekly progress. Make sure that all of the necessary equipment is available for presentations.

- **Agenda**. Check that there is an agenda and that it is circulated in advance. For ad hoc meetings it is recommended that you first agree on an agenda.
- **Invitation**. Make sure that all attendees know the time and date, place and agenda in advance. Make sure that essential attendees can be there or reschedule.
- **Minutes and notes**. Whilst formal minutes of every meeting are neither appropriate nor needed, every meeting should result in a list of actions, with time limits that can be followed up. Make sure that this happens and that a copy is available for the file. Failure to do this can result in chaos.
- **Actions**. If there are no minutes then one person must make sure that any actions allocated are recorded, communicated to the person given the action and accepted by that person.

KEY POINT

Take notes. Whenever you meet with a supplier keep a written record of what was agreed; get them to agree that it is accurate at the end of the meeting or shortly afterwards to make sure you have a common understanding of what was said.

SALES AND BUYING TECHNIQUES

Although there is an instant guide to negotiating in Chapter 10 for those needing the basics, it is worth pointing out some of the common strategies used by suppliers. Forearmed is forewarned here, although you are more likely to find the more aggressive tactics at the volume or commodity end of the market. Where a supplier is building a long-term relationship with you they need to work as partners rather than as market traders. That said these are selling basics; you will find them in your local shop. The retail world uses all of the sales mechanisms that you find in the 'more sophisticated' IT solutions sales world, they are just packaged differently. Keep in mind that just because these are sales techniques it does not mean they are going to harm your business if you buy. Just be careful to make sure you are getting a good deal on something you actually need.

NOTE

It may seem like a joke, but you can find many of the basic sales tricks in Ronnie Barker's 1970s television series *Open All Hours*, available on DVD and regularly shown on satellite television channels.

FUD

This stands for fear, uncertainty and doubt. It is one of the oldest tricks in the book: all insurance companies use it on a daily basis. Credit card companies prey on your fear of identity fraud to get you to choose their card. It also is one of the most common tactics used by those selling electrical and domestic appliances and is seen in the form of the 'extended warranty'. In engineering terms this warranty is almost certainly a con. Figure 9.1 shows the 'bathtub' curve which links reliability with product life.

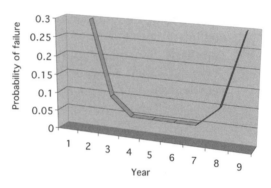

FIGURE 9.1 *The 'bathtub' curve that links reliability with product life*

Things are most likely to break when they are new or at the end of their working life. The extended warranty covers the most reliable phase so is at a low risk to the insurer and hence very profitable. The client is sold the warranty on the basis of piece of mind: only a few pence a day to know it will be fixed if it goes wrong. What you need to know is how likely it is to go wrong versus the actual cost of fixing it. An extended warranty over a couple of years can cost more than a new unit.

The smaller SME is likely to come across this tactic when buying anything from retail IT store. It is commonly sold with printers, PCs and network equipment.

KEY POINT

Only buy an extended warranty if the failure of the device is mission critical and you cannot afford to just go out and replace it quickly. This also applies to buying any insurance: only buy it if you cannot afford not to.

There are many other versions of FUD in use. In the 1960s and 1970s it was rumoured that 'nobody ever got fired for buying IBM' was a tactic used to persuade large corporate organisation decision makers to choose their product: the safe option. Some variations on the theme are listed in Table 9.1.

TABLE 9.1   *Variations on FUD*

Example	Comment
'Buy now while we have it in stock.'	Someone else will have it in stock too.
'We have another customer keen to buy, so if you want it you need to say now.'	Again they are unlikely to be the only source, let them sell it.
'Wouldn't you like to have the peace of mind knowing that the warranty will last three years if you pay for the extension?'	How long do you expect to have your IT kit before it needs updating anyway?
'This price can't be held for much longer.'	No, it will be cheaper next week.

The related sale

A classic example is for the sales assistant to sell you toothpaste to go with your new toothbrush. You will find this technique in use in all retail computer stores: buy a printer and they will offer you spare toner or reams of paper; buy a computer and they will offer you a printer, a home network or an internet connection. This is a simple and reliable technique; it is proven that it works. The key to its success is that they are selling you something you are likely to need. You only need to be cautious about the price and take time to think if you already have whatever it is back in the office.

The next step up from this in the IT world is to sell related training: you buy word processing and spreadsheet applications, do your staff need related training? This can extend further than you might think: time management training might be something that could be sold on the back of office productivity software.

Moving on to more complex IT procurements, the opportunities for the related sale increase still further. Training, security, networking, data storage, disaster recovery, personal skills, temporary staff, the list goes on; these can all be promoted on the back of your original requirement. This is not a bad thing, just be aware that it will happen and make informed decisions.

Extras

Particularly when buying items such as PCs it is a good idea to make sure that you know what is or is not included. The author knows from personal experience that comparing one PC with another can take almost more time than any savings you may make are worth. Obvious examples include VAT (included or not), monitor (included or not, size of screen etc.), what applications software or version of the operating system is bundled with the PC, warranty cover (onsite, return to base, how long etc.), delivery and installation.

Some suppliers make it easier than others to understand what you are getting for your money. With website-based suppliers the simplest thing, although time-consuming, is to go through the complete configuration exercise online, choosing what you want, then seeing what the final price is. Then you can compare like with like, or at least similar with similar: not all suppliers offer the same options.

Whatever you are buying it is up to you to make sure that everything you need is included in the price you pay.

Overselling

This is a bit like the car salesman who sells you an estate car because 'you never know when you need to move a big load, perhaps taking garden rubbish to the tip...' when what you really needed was a runabout to get you to the supermarket once a week.

The IT equivalent of this is being sold a PC or a server that has more storage and processor power than you actually need to do the job. Fortunately in the case of a PC this is unlikely to make a huge difference: you may pay twice as much, but twice as much is still not very much money today. In the case of servers there is more scope for expense and you could be looking at significant increases in cost for no benefit.

CASE STUDY

One London-based SME with about 12 users decided to upgrade from networked PCs (on a simple LAN) to a server plus networked PCs. They went to a small local supplier who they had used for their LAN and PC maintenance and applications supply since they were formed a couple of years before. They had a good relationship with them and felt they understood what was required. The new server performed well and all seemed fine. However, as a result of growth they moved to a different part of London and the support organisation was no longer as close. As they needed a four-hour response on faults and travel in London would make that hard for the existing supplier to guarantee, a new supplier was sought. They supplied potential service organisations with an inventory of their hardware and software. One of the organisations asked why they had such a powerful server. It turned out that they could support over 100 users on their equipment. This was taking space to grow a bit far. In financial terms this had made a hole in the bottom line in both capital spend and ongoing support costs, power usage and so on. They felt upset that they had been oversold by the original service provider. They took future business elsewhere.

However, this is not always the supplier's fault: miscommunication and misunderstanding can cause the supplier to aim on the side of caution.

If they are not sure exactly how the system is to be used they may err on the side of caution rather than have complaints about performance.

KEY POINT

To avoid being oversold be specific about what you want and get more than one quotation for comparison. Even if you do not understand the answer, ask what the basis is for sizing equipment.

Being entertained

There are suppliers who try and win business simply on the basis of giving you meals, tickets to the opera, air shows, concerts and so forth. This may be very nice for you, but it is no substitute for a professional working relationship with a supplier you trust and respect. Be cautious about companies that are over keen to do this. Somebody has to pay and by implication it is their customers, including you. There is no such thing as the proverbial free lunch; keep that in mind.

How many suppliers?

This is really aimed at those making regular purchases, for example of consumables and small items. When you are procuring a system or something bespoke then you will be choosing a supplier for that specific job. For the smaller purchase of commodity items (and this includes PCs and printers) you have a wide choice of supplier. Consequently it is tempting to shop around for each purchase on the grounds of getting a better deal. However, this can get out of hand for anything more than occasional purchases by a sole trader. The more suppliers you have the more admin you will have to go with them. There is a real cost for this in terms of keeping track of it all and, if anything goes wrong, you will need to sort out what you bought from whom and have the proof of purchase. The author's suggestion is that unless the savings are huge or you are very tight for money, then for most businesses it is worth having a local, preferred supplier. After a trial period to see how you get on you might want to look at having an account as monthly billing and payment periods will provide a cash flow benefit that can easily offset any small price savings gained by shopping around. It will also save you time.

An additional benefit of keeping the number of suppliers limited is that you stand a better chance of building a relationship with them. This can pay dividends in terms of their better understanding of your business and the improved service this can lead to.

This is particularly relevant when buying consumables. You can always find a better deal on anything if you put time and effort into it.

KEY POINT

There are hidden costs in shopping around and continually switching suppliers: you should ask yourself how much time are you willing to spend to save £5 on a toner cartridge.

CHECKLIST

We provide here a checklist of items to review when considering a supplier.

Is the supplier financially stable (at least for as long as you want the equipment or service)?   ☐

Can they provide you with the support and service you need?   ☐

Do they have the equipment in stock?   ☐

Can they meet your delivery timetable?   ☐

Have you established a working relationship with them already?   ☐

Can they provide relevant references from people you trust?   ☐

Do they treat you as an important client?   ☐

Do you like the people you are dealing with and do you get on?   ☐

Do you really want them to quote?   ☐

SUMMARY

Choosing your supplier, whether it is for buying a new cartridge for an inkjet printer or for a complete million pound plus service solution, can be critical to having a happy ending. The working relationship you build with them certainly will be. There will be those reading this who take an entirely exploitative approach to their business relationships, who will be sneering at the philosophy behind the win–win approach described here. Not paying invoices, 'forgetting' to sign the cheque or shouting abuse down the phone can only offer short-term gains. Such people may be interested to know that history is not on their side: organisations that value their supply chain have a better track record of longevity and profitability.

Treat your supplier as you would wish your customers to treat you, but also demand the same respect and flexibility from them.

10 Negotiation

Here we give an introduction to negotiation skills with an emphasis on win–win strategies and maintaining long-term supplier relationships.

INTRODUCTION

This is the only specific skills training chapter in the book. It is included because despite the availability of many excellent books on the subject (see the references and further reading for some examples), negotiation is an essential part of any procurement. It also follows on naturally from the previous chapter on suppliers and it is suggested that the two are read together if practical. This overview and basic training guide is included so that the book can function as a standalone guide for the SME IT buyer.

> **KEY POINT**
>
> Everything is negotiable. Whatever you want can always be traded off against something you are not so keen on; price is not the only issue.

NEGOTIATION CYCLE

First of all we present some theory that describes what actually happens during a negotiation. There is a five-step cycle (see Figure 10.1) that can be used to describe the progression of a negotiation. The steps are plan, explore, offer, barter and close (at which point it starts again). The stages are briefly described here to serve as an introduction to negotiation.

FIGURE 10.1   *The negotiation cycle*

Plan (the starting point)

This is spilt into two sections: prioritising and knowing the audience.

Prioritising

Before getting started it is important to know what you want to achieve. Make a list of what you need and then put priorities on it. The high-priority items should include only the things you cannot do without, for example you may need a minimum of three PCs for your staff to access your stock control system. The medium priorities are things you would like to have and are of significant benefit but are not essential, for instance a spare PC would help with peak loads on the stock control system and would save having to pay overtime for someone to come in on a Saturday morning to catch up. The low-priority items are 'would be nice' but really do not matter too much. A possible example in this case might be a colour printer instead of a black and white one for stock reports. When you have done this you know where to draw the line and what you can sacrifice without affecting the success of your procurement. Remember that your priority may not be the same as the suppliers. Perhaps the supplier has a number of PCs in stock that are not easy to sell (last year's model) and are costing them money on the shelf. One of these PCs would be sufficient for your spare PC and you might get this at a low price: they have traded a higher priority need for your medium priority requirement.

Knowing your audience

In other words, whom are you negotiating with? People's roles make a difference to how they will negotiate and what matters to them. It is important to know if the person or people you are dealing with directly are those who will make the decision or influencers of that decision. For example you may be dealing with the technical people who are helping to specify your system or application, whereas decisions on pricing are likely to be made by sales or financial staff. This will influence how you negotiate.

NOTE

Decision makers sign cheques, agree deals, put their name to the contract and close the deal. Influencers are their advisers: they are involved in the decision but do not actually take final responsibility for the outcome.

Explore

This is where investing time pays dividends: do not be in a hurry or try to cut corners. Once you know whom you are dealing with and what you want (outputs from the plan step) it is tempting to start negotiating on the spot. Do not do this; explore the options and talk to the other people involved. Ask open questions, those without yes or no answers (for example, 'what will make delivery easy for you?'). You want to find out what they want, show that you understand their priorities and build rapport if possible. Whilst this progresses make sure that what is discussed is summarised, otherwise there is a danger that you will start negotiating for different things. The purpose of these early discussions is to gauge the other party's views, create an open dialogue and check your understanding and any preconceptions you might have. It is also a chance to reduce tension and build rapport. In many cases this step takes up to 80% of the time for any negotiation; however, as already mentioned this is time well spent.

Offer

Do not start this step until you can summarise what the other side wants and have a clear understanding of what you want. This is where many people think negotiation really starts. Here each side needs to make the starting position clear, stating what they want. You must leave yourself room for manoeuvre here: if you start with your bottom line figure then there is nowhere for you to go. Also do not mention all of the options open to you, for example the secondary low- and medium-priority items you may want to throw into the pot later. You want the 'if–then' approach available where you offer something extra on condition that the other side offers something else. For example, 'If we spilt the order in two, can we have the first notebooks earlier?'.

Barter

Following on from offer, this is the real haggling stage and is akin to the street trader offering to throw in a bag of carrots if you buy two sacks of potatoes. What you do here is critical. There is a golden rule, 'never give anything away without asking for something in return'. This is 'if–then' again, for example, 'If we agree to sign up for a year's technical support after the warranty period expires can we have free onsite hardware cover for the first six months after delivery?' It is useful if you can link items, then they can be bargained off against each other, in this case post-sales support. Things can get very complicated when you are trading off one thing against another, so it essential that you take notes so that you know where you are. This is doubly important if this stage takes place over more than one meeting: you need to know exactly what was on offer before.

Close

This is the final stage. A deal has been struck and there is a definition of what is going to happen. Document this and make sure you cover all of the important details. This is necessary because after it is documented both sides can read it and agree that it correctly defines the deal. In addition it serves as an audit trail to reduce the chances of future disputes over who said or agreed to what. It is essential that a full stop should be put on negotiations at this stage; if there are any signs that the whole process is about to start up again, be prepared to stand your ground.

WHAT TO NEGOTIATE

The following sections describe items that you are likely to negotiate in a procurement. Keep in mind that you need to consider all negotiable items as an overall package: do not lose sight of the overall cost of ownership when considering an individual item.

Payment terms

The most obvious being 'how much?', the next being 'when?'. You can always offer a supplier a smaller sum than they are asking for and see what happens: they can always say no. You can also suggest staged payments or instalments. For anything that is at all project based you should negotiate staged payments that are linked to successful delivery: do not pay everything upfront.

Volume

Working on the principle that there are economies of scale then the more you buy the better the price you will get. For example if you buy five laser printers at the same time you ought to get a reduction in unit and shipping costs. Buying consumables such as paper, toner or inkjet cartridges are good areas to look for volume discounts.

You may also be able to get volume discounts based on the financial volume of goods you buy from a supplier. For instance if you exceed more than £5,000 in one year you might get a reduction in the form of a payback or credit against further orders.

> **NOTE**
>
> There are limits to this for an SME: you are unlikely to want to buy 1,000 PCs. However, it may be worth getting together with other local firms to look at volume buying for some items.

Warranties

Most hardware items purchased new come with some form of warranty. If you have your own support contract for your equipment already then you might be able to save some money by asking the supplier to 'unbundle' the warranty, in other words sell you the equipment without the warranty.

You might also be able to negotiate more favourable terms on warranty if you are buying several identical items.

Service levels

The level of service you get can have a significant impact on the price for delivering that service. It is much more expensive to send an engineer to a site to repair something than it is to fix it back at base. This is why onsite support costs more than return to base. Onsite costs also vary with the speed of response required: next day is much cheaper than a four-hour response.

You can balance what you need with what you can afford. You can also revisit what is on offer and look for reductions in price against a lower level of service, perhaps choosing to leave non-critical items out of onsite support. Related to this is the negotiation of penalty clauses for non-performance: what will the consequence be for the supplier if they do not meet contracted support levels? This applies to any service you might purchase, not just the hardware maintenance examples given here.

Performance and capacity

Performance and capacity are often key issues when looking at IT systems. How much capacity (usually in terms of disk space) and performance (in terms of CPU speed and memory) you have makes a difference in price. There will always be a trade-off available to you that relates to these elements.

Time

When do you want it? Usually the longer you are prepared to wait for something the lower the cost is likely to be. Also if you are prepared to fit in with a supplier's 'slacker' times and fit in with their need to fill bigger high-priority orders then they may be able to reduce your price. You can only do this if you have that flexibility, but time is always a good thing to negotiate.

An exception to this is when a supplier has something in stock or people available instantly for which they have no buyer. They may be willing to give a good rate if you take it 'today'; however, see also 'FUD' in sales tactics both in this chapter and in Chapter 9: the 'it'll be gone by tomorrow' ploy.

Priorities

Another variation on time to some extent. By looking at the priorities of different parts of a procurement, or number of procurements, you can decide which things you want most urgently. You can then negotiate down to a budget by putting off the less-urgent items or choosing those that provide the quickest return on investment. The other items can then be purchased when funds permit.

Resources

Both the buyer and the seller will have resource limitations: few businesses (particularly SMEs) have spare staff today. Consequently there will always be opportunities to negotiate in this area. It can be as trivial as disposing of the packaging yourself instead of insisting that the supplier does it. It might be a case of supplying a resource to the supplier post-sale to help define requirements in exchange for a reduced price.

> **NOTE**
>
> In the more 'M' sized organisations the person managing the procurement may well find that they have to negotiate for internal resources. The techniques and strategies here work just as well in this case too.

Publicity

Just as double-glazing companies may offer a discount if they can use your building as a show house for their work then some suppliers may offer a discount for publicity. This is really only likely for bespoke developments and service or system suppliers: do not expect to do this if you just buy a PC. This might be in the form of an agreement to use your name on brochures; it might be a press launch for a new system. A spin-off of any such deal is that the supplier has an added incentive to make it work.

> **KEY POINT**
>
> Negotiation and dispute resolution strategies are much the same: you are trying to reach a common understanding.

NEGOTIATION STRATEGIES

There are many ways to go about a negotiation. Given that you are reading this it is assumed that you are not a professional negotiator so here are the basics. You can use any of these and in different situations may need all of them. However, for long-term business relationships some work better than others.

Win–lose

One party aims to win at all costs, irrespective of the impact and expense to the other side. This can only work where there is an absolute point that cannot be negotiated or there is no intention of ever working with the other side ever again. Most SMEs dealing with IT suppliers will want an ongoing relationship if possible. IT is often an essential part of the business and you do not want to put its support in peril. You might consider using this when buying commodities if you are really desperate to save the last penny. When interviewing SME people for this book nobody suggested this approach: however, it is still in use, including by a minority of suppliers.

> **NOTE**
>
> A milder example of this is an old trick from the manufacturing industry. The trick is to negotiate hard over, say, 100 units, then when you have the best price and seem about to sign, ask for the price for 1,000.

> **KEY POINT**
>
> There is one time when you should follow this strategy. If the only deal on offer to you is unacceptable then the maxim is 'no deal is better than a bad deal'. You could argue that this is a lose–lose deal, but never make a deal that does not meet your minimum requirements because you feel anything is better than nothing. Go away and think about it further.

Delay

This strategy is more positive than win–lose; the opportunity to use delay as a tactic is limited by the time available until you need the goods or services involved. It may be that you adopt this approach rather than accept a bad deal (see the note under win–lose). The strategy is to put off the negotiation to a future date in the hope that a better deal will emerge. The problem with this is that it can only be used when it does not matter if there is a delay in making the purchase. Take the example of a bulk order for laser printer toner: you cannot put it off if you are down to your last half of a cartridge and will need to print a set of flyers next week.

> **NOTE**
>
> When this strategy is adopted it is important to set a timetable for when the negotiation must be resumed. Do not leave things dangling or the supplier may go away or forget about you.

Look at both sides

This is more of a technique than a strategy as it gathers information rather than making an offer to negotiate. It is only part of an overall strategy and is closely related to the 'explore' stage of the negotiation cycle. The goal is to understand both sides of the deal and make sure that all key points are summarised and agreed. Then both you and the supplier know where you are. It is also worth applying this at any stage in the negotiation when there is any chance of a misunderstanding.

Co-operation

A logical follow on from 'look at both sides'; start this by establishing a common understanding of each other's situation and respect the different viewpoints. Starting a negotiation from here means that there is a common understanding and foundation for fair bargaining. You are showing each other that you will accommodate the other party's needs as well as trying to meet your own. As with 'look at both sides' this is only part of the story, you are mainly establishing the basis for the negotiation. For example you might need to have equipment installed outside working hours so as not to interrupt work for your clients. Your supplier may not have staff on hand who can do this during the week, but might be able to do the work on a Saturday. This might mean that it takes longer to complete this installation, but it could allow the supplier to work around your requirement so as not to inconvenience your paying customers.

The win–win deal: finding a solution

From the author's experience this is the best strategy of all, particularly for IT procurement. The underlying principle is to work together to find a joint solution to the problem to be solved and so complete the deal. As an example you might want your systems installed on Wednesday but your supplier has a problem with staff availability due to sickness. You could insist that they hire a contract resource at their own expense to meet your deadline. This is a win–lose deal that might be good in the short term but certainly will not predispose the supplier to help you out in the future. A compromise might be that the supplier does the installation over the weekend, later than you wanted but perhaps without the disruption to daily working of the original plan. The supplier might avoid extra costs and you might end up with less lost revenue from the reduced disruption. More importantly you have solved a problem together and learnt about each other's business, something you can both benefit from in the future.

WHAT WORKS BEST?

To some extent it is horses for courses. There are times when a take it or leave it approach is necessary: this may lead to a win–lose situation that could damage or even prevent future trading. For example you may have been delivered equipment that is simply too unreliable to continue with.

CASE STUDY

An ex-IT-specialist had set up a training business. After a couple of years he decided to buy a new PC and, wanting something special, he went to a company that produced bespoke systems. This was an organisation with a good reputation that had been recommended. Once delivered the machine proved to be prone to breakdown and crashing. It went back to the suppliers a number of times and various fixes were supplied. It never actually settled down and after several months he decided to call a halt to proceedings and request his money back. To the firms credit they, somewhat reluctantly, agreed to this. However, this was very much a case of that is it, we will not trade again, a feeling held by both parties after what was a long-running dispute. This was a lose–lose transaction.

The case study is an extreme case; in general it usually works out best if both parties are happy or at least neutral. You want to be in the position where both parties are happy with the deal they got and are happy to trade again. For SMEs word of mouth is even more important than it is for larger organisations. In fact word of mouth is about the only free advertising you will get. The way you negotiate and the way you resolve the inevitable disputes that occur will establish the reputation you deserve.

CASE STUDY

A training organisation provided communications (human, not technical) skills training. They needed a new office system (a handful of PCs, printers, network and the like). As they had limited technical expertise they needed not just the equipment and software but installation and training too. One supplier offered a reasonable price on the equipment but was not able to offer the training. Other suppliers seemed to be more expensive for the equipment, but were able to offer the training. The training organisation asked the reasonably priced supplier why (**explore**) they did not offer training: 'Do you not have the technical knowledge?' It turned out that they did, but had very little training expertise and had made a mess of training in the past. An offer was made (**offer**) to provide a one-day training course on how to train in exchange for free installation and user training. After some debate on pricing for the equipment and the location for the training course (**barter**) this was accepted by the supplier (**close**). Not only was this a happy outcome for the initial deal, but also led to occasional spin-off business for both parties, including a sales presentations course. This was not only a win–win situation but generated long-term future business for both.

Consider all of the strategies described but keep in mind that you are in business for the long term, at least if you want to survive. Choose accordingly.

'DO'S' AND 'DON'TS' OF CLOSING A DEAL

We present a list of 'do's' and 'don'ts' when closing a deal in Table 10.1.

TABLE 10.1   *The 'do's' and 'don'ts' of closing a deal*

Do	Don't
Decide when to stop: do not risk opening things up again.	**Go on too long**, because you will open things up again.
Write down what is agreed: if you do not then the deal is not really closed; it is a matter of opinion.	**Get euphoric**: it is too easy to get carried away and start offering new goodies whilst under the influence of an excess of goodwill.
Bluff with your final offer.	**Make closing concessions.**
Clarify all agreements: it is important that all parties properly understand the deal. Even if it is written down, if people did not understand it they may try and go back on it. Worse, they may even feel that they were deliberately misled.	**Use loose definitions**: they make it hard to know what the actual deal is and it will not stick.
Make benefit statements that show how everyone wins from the deal. Make sure these are clearly understood.	**Dither**: a decision has to be made one way or the other.
Stick to your finish position: once the deal is made do not restart the negotiation again.	**Cheat**: you will get found out and then you will not be trusted to deal with again.
End on a win–win note: it is important that the deal is seen to be good for all concerned. This will help cement the agreement and have a beneficial effect on future negotiations.	**Disclose your real bottom line**: if you do then you either leave the other side feeling cheated if you have agreed on more or leave yourself with nowhere to go.
Look forward to the next deal.	**Lose your objective**: there was a reason you went into this negotiation, do not forget it in the thrill of the deal.

NOTE

This can be seen from the point of view of the buyer or the seller. When it comes down to it both sides of the procurement are looking to obtain a result: closing the deal.

CHECKLIST

We provide here a checklist of key points to consider for any negotiation.

Have you defined what your minimum
acceptable requirement or price is? ☐

Have you defined the highest price
you are willing to pay? ☐

Have you kept your minimum deal or
bottom line position to yourself? ☐

What are the negotiable items for the deal? ☐

What are your 'must haves', 'would likes'
and 'no big deal' negotiable items? ☐

Have you considered what is the best
strategy for this negotiation? ☐

What will deliver you and the
supplier a win–win trade? ☐

SUMMARY

During the latter stages of any procurement there will always be a need to negotiate. If you do not haggle then you are probably paying too much. There can be a large number of negotiable items involved in an IT procurement, take the time to look at what they are before you get to the end game of the deal. Once you have them identified and have your baseline position identified for each of them you can negotiate from a sound position.

When it comes down to strategy the best option is usually the win–win deal: for IT you want a long-term relationship with your supplier. The short-term benefits of getting a cut-throat price at someone else's expense may appeal to the ego, but as an SME you do not have the weight to demand people do business with you if you upset them. You do not have the stranglehold over suppliers that a supermarket might have. Any short-term wins will leave you without friendly suppliers when you need them.

11 Legal Issues

Here we describe what to consider, when to get professional help and so forth: not specific legal advice, just things to look out for. Licences, intellectual property and due diligence are also discussed.

INTRODUCTION

As any procurement is going to involve a contractual relationship between a client and the supplier(s), even if it is not put in writing, then it is foolhardy of anybody not to take legal issues into account. It would be equally foolhardy for the author to offer legal advice, not only due to lack of legal expertise but also because we live in litigious times, particularly on the western side of the Atlantic. So now is the time for a disclaimer.

> ### DISCLAIMER
>
> The author and the publishers accept no liability for the consequences of any action or lack of action taken by the reader because they have relied on this chapter in place of, or in addition to, obtaining professional legal guidance.

The purpose of this chapter is to identify some of the areas where you may need professional advice: it is not to be seen as a substitute for that advice. When in doubt, get a professional opinion; you have been warned. In particular the reader's attention is brought to the horrendous minefield that is the software licence; more on this including a rant and a plea for better times is given later.

WHAT TO CONSIDER?

In procurement terms there are a number of areas to think about: your own responsibilities and liabilities; the supplier's responsibilities and liabilities; T&Cs for payments; service levels; warranties; and guarantees.

Your first step is to start with this list and ask yourself whether you understand what your position is with regard to these points. If there are gaps, then you should investigate further.

SOFTWARE LICENCES

This is really is a topic that could fill a book (albeit a rather dull one) in itself. Although the topic is dull the consequences of getting it wrong can be interesting, in terms of financial hardship and no comeback on faulty software or the consequences of using it. A major part of the problem is that such licences are invariably written in anything but plain English.

Basic principle

The concept behind software licences is based on that of literary copyright. You buy the right to use the software, but you do not own the intellectual property. So far, so good, but most software licences are far more restrictive than the T&Cs that apply when you buy a book. For example many ban resale; some only rent you the software for a period of time, you do not own anything other than the right to use it for a while. Furthermore by the time you have read all of the small print you may well find that the supplier can withdraw the right to use it at any time, makes no guarantee that it will work and certainly is not responsible for any loss or problems you may have as a result of using it.

> **KEY POINT**
>
> Most software licences only give you the right to use the software within strictly defined boundaries. It is not yours to do with as you please or to modify.

Variations

No two licences seem to be the same and no two manufacturers seem to have similar approaches to licensing. For example one supplier may licence on a per-machine basis, another on a per-user basis: a single-use licence can have very different meanings. The per-machine example may mean that if you buy a new PC you need to buy a whole new licence whilst the per-user licence might not.

It can get even more confusing with multiple-user licences. Table 11.1 gives a few variations on a theme for a five-user licence; it should provide an idea of what to expect.

TABLE 11.1   *Variations on a theme for a five-user licence*

Variation	Possible interpretation
Five-machine licence	You can have five copies of the software installed on separate computers (you probably have to register each machine). Who uses the machines is not important.
Five-user licence (named users)	Only five people who you have registered may use this software, nobody else can (e.g. sick leave cover may be an issue).
Five-user licence (maximum)	Up to five people, whoever they are, can use the application: they may be on any machine with access to the software.

(Continued)

TABLE 11.1 *(Continued)*

Variation	Possible interpretation
Five-user licence (concurrent)	Here you can have any number of users but only five of them are allowed to use it at any one time (typically this would be for a server-based application where there is a mechanism for enforcing it, but not always). You might have 30 people but only five at a time should use it.
Five-user licence (single site)	You can have five users (however defined, see options in this table) but only at one site.
Five-user licence (multiple sites)	Again, you can have five users but spread over a number of sites.
Five-user licence (one year)	Could be any of the above but limits your use to 12 months after which you need to pay again. You may have no control over next year's price.
Five-user upgrade	An upgrade from a smaller licence (e.g. single user) to support more users. This will raise the question on a time-limited licence as to when it runs out if it depends on the original single-user licence for validity.

As if this was not enough, in the corporate sector there are major issues regarding licence requirements where 'virtualised' servers are employed.

> **KEY POINT**
>
> Software licensing is so complex that is it routinely ignored in many SMEs: they risk large fines and punitive legal action, often without knowing it and often without deliberately setting out to cheat the supplier.

Commercial software

Here the software is a commercial, copyright product, a little like a book: you can read it, but you do not own the copyright. This analogy should not be stretched too far. With a book you can usually sell it on second hand or allow someone else to read it. With computer software this is often not the case. Commercial software is intended generate revenue for the developer or owner.

Your right to use

As mentioned earlier in this chapter the normal terms of a licence only provide you with the right to use the software within certain restrictions.

Intellectual property

In a book the intellectual property is the content of the cook: you cannot copy it and pass it off as your own, it is the intellectual property that is copyrighted. The intellectual property of software will include both the source code and the code that you run on the computer. See also the section on terms to watch out for later in this chapter. It is important to be aware of who owns the intellectual property for any software that is produced specially for you: you need to know you can continue to use it and you should have control over who else may be allowed to use it.

Open source

There is a significant open-source software community in existence. One of the best examples of open-source software is OpenOffice (www.openoffice.org). This is available free to download and use as you will; the 'open source' refers to the availability of the source code itself to help with support and to encourage the development of new components.

It is important to note that this is still copyrighted material: you cannot pirate chunks of this code and sell it on as your own (at least not legally).

Free software

Even if you are using freeware or open-source software for which there is no charge there will be licensing terms in force. Your rights are controlled even if you get it for free. In particular you will not be allowed to sell it on for profit. You may not be able to pass it on for free without acknowledging the author's copyright.

KEY POINT

Freeware that is for non-commercial use may not legally be used for your business. Also software that is supplied free for an evaluation period may become illegal if used after the agreed period.

Shareware

The first thing to understand is that shareware is not free. The concept behind shareware is that of marketing on a try before you buy basis. One of the best-known examples of shareware and probably the most abused is the well-known WinZip range of data compression products (see www.winzip.com). This is commonly used to compress files for transmission via modem or WAN connections. It is distributed on many magazine CDs and DVDs and widely on websites. Many people use this on an evaluation basis for years on end. In fact after the evaluation period you are supposed to buy a licence (typically $20–30 at the time of writing).

Licensing checklist

Questions to ask yourself or the supplier about any software licences are given in Table 11.2.

TABLE 11.2   *Licensing checklist*

Question	Comment
What is the supplier giving you?	Get them to explain what you are getting and how changes may affect you.
Are you clear how many licences you need or will receive?	Make sure that the licences you have fit the real pattern of use you expect, e.g. everyone who needs to can use it including any casual staff you employ.
Do you understand any constraints that apply, e.g. for changes?	If the standard offering does not do what you require do you have the right to modify it (keep in mind that if you do, then future releases of the product may not work with your add-ons)?
Do you know how long the licence lasts for?	Some are time limited, for example 12 months. What will happen at the end of that time, are you at risk from price hikes?
What happens if they go out of business?	Are there arrangements to allow you to continue using the software if they become insolvent, cease trading etc.?
Are you happy with the arrangements?	If there are any niggling doubts, ask before not after purchase.

A rant and a plea

The author would like to complain about the horrendously complex and obfuscatory language that is used in most software licences, indeed in almost every legal item that applies to IT. Much of the blame for this lies with the USA's legal system, product liability law and consequent blame culture. It would be so nice, even if they do need to cover themselves (and they do need to), if they could include a plain English summary of the basics of what you can and cannot do with what you have paid money for, even if they had to include a huge disclaimer saying that this is just for starters.

The author has had personal experience of the terrible complexities that can occur with licences for large organisations when they are taken over or merge. There are instances where entire multimillion-pound deals have been put at risk or abandoned because of the complexity of the licensing. It does not have to be this difficult but presumably it is more profitable because it is.

KEY POINT

The author would have liked to include a copy of a popular product's licence in an appendix and have it marked up where it really bites you. Sadly the licence itself was subject to copyright and could not be reproduced.

FAST

It is worth giving a mention to the Federation Against Software Theft (FAST) here. This was the world's first anti-piracy organisation working to protect the intellectual property of software publishers. It was formed in 1984 and its initial remit was to lobby Parliament for changes in the law which resulted in 'a computer program' being included in the definition of a 'literary work' in the Copyright, Designs and Patents Act 1988. Although lobbying is still part of the FAST's aim its activities have broadened over the years such that it now addresses the misuse, overuse and theft of software intellectual property in the following ways:

- utilising civil and criminal processes;
- lobbying Parliament to strengthen the provisions of the Copyright, Designs and Patents Act including increasing director's liability under the act;
- educating organisations through the FAST Standard for Software Compliance (FSSC1-2004);
- education through schools and universities;
- increasing awareness of software intellectual property theft within the user community by a continual programme of press, television and radio interviews and articles.

Their website www.fast.org.uk contains much useful information.

WARRANTIES

Hardware

Most equipment comes with some form of warranty or guarantee that it will work for a minimum period. This is typically 12 months for something like a PC, a printer or a router (you may be able to purchase extended options on this or a superior warranty). At the basic level it will be a 'return to base' warranty where it is up to you at your own cost to return the faulty goods for them to repair or replace. You may be without the item for a while. A higher level of warranty may be one where they collect and return the item, but you are still without the item whilst it is fixed. Better still is an onsite warranty where they send an engineer who will fix it there and then or offer a replacement. These superior warranties will come with a price tag (for a PC this may be a significant fraction of the value): you need to make a business case for such a service. You can also choose to extend the warranty for a number of years (see the next section for a discussion on the value of this).

It is important to know what a warranty does and does not include. For example it might include normal wear and tear, but it will probably not include accidental damage, deliberate damage or misuse. For this reason you are always advised to include any new equipment on your insurance policies: there have been examples where people mistakenly relied on a warranty in lieu of proper insurance. This is a bad idea for obvious reasons.

There may be an option to pay less for the equipment if you 'unbundled' the warranty. You reduce the supplier's liability to 'dead on delivery'; in other words once you have accepted it and agreed it works then it is up to you to deal with the faults yourself. This option comes in handy if you have a maintenance contract that covers all of your equipment: you simply notify your maintainer about the new kit and subject to their agreement and pricing arrangements it becomes their problem. This does mean that they have some say in what you buy: they need to be able to support it with their existing spares, engineering support and so forth. Also it must be of an acceptable quality that is not likely to fall to bits too easily.

Extended warranties on equipment

Although covered elsewhere the topic of extended warranties, mainly sold at retail outlets, is worth another brief mention here. These are normally insurance policies rather than an actual warranty supplied by the manufacturer. They usually cover between one and three years further support in case of product failure. Treat them with caution: they are taking advantage of the 'bathtub' curve. Products are most likely to fail either in the short period of use after initial manufacture or towards the end of their design life. The bit in the middle (the flat part of the bathtub) holds the lowest risk of failure. It is this period that extended warranties cover. For this reason they are often very poor value: treat them with caution. This is particularly true for return to base services where you do not have the added value of an engineer visiting your site.

Software

For off-the-shelf software the manufacturers supply little if any warranty; it is hard to find another industry where products are supplied with so little guarantee as to function. For office applications and PC utility or operating software this rarely proves to be an issue; provided that the suppliers are well known you are unlikely to have major issues.

For bespoke software or tailored applications that are critical to running your business you may wish to have something more substantial in place (see the section on terms to watch out for below). Similarly where people operate services on your behalf, for example operating servers for you or providing communications networks, it is reasonable to expect some form of warranty as to their operation. Usually you would want to incorporate this into some form of ongoing supply and support, embodied in a SLA. You should discuss and negotiate a suitable agreement for this with the supplier that represents your business risk.

SERVICE LEVEL AGREEMENTS

As mentioned earlier these are important documents for any critical service or bespoke supply. They form the basis of the service to be delivered, how it is measured and penalties or rewards for failing or exceeding agreed metrics. As such they need to cover all aspects of the service you require including hours of cover, response times, locations, how the service is measured, helpdesks, technical support, penalties for non-delivery, what is required from you and so forth.

SLAs commonly include segments to address a definition of services, performance measurement, problem management, customer duties, warranties, disaster recovery and termination of agreement. It is a very important document and if you get it right it will be able to:

- reduce potential areas for conflict;
- set achievable and realistic expectations;
- identify and define what is to be delivered and what is needed;
- define a framework for understanding and for governance;
- provide the vehicle for two-way communication to resolve disputes;
- make complex issues clear and understandable in simple terms.

SLA structure and components

A typical SLA might include the sections described below. The exact structure and nature of an SLA will be dependent on the specific requirements, however, this gives an idea as to the scope and content to be expected. This is roughly compatible with the structure suggested by what is regarded as the industry 'best practice' ITIL (Stationary Office Books 2005). Note that the SLA is sometimes a separate schedule to a main contract; sometimes it is all part of the main contract. For this reason some sections listed here may or may not be present (they are also covered in the later section on terms to watch out for).

Introduction

This will include a brief overview of the service, context and information about the structure of the SLA.

Services to be delivered or service description

This section should cover what you are going to get (e.g. helpdesk support, onsite visits from engineers and so forth), the impact of success or failure of the service element and business priorities. It is essential that you understand what this section means: if you do not, ask for further explanation and documentation until you do.

Service hours

This is quite simply when the service will be available: 09:00 to 17:00, Monday to Friday excluding public holidays might be classed as 'normal' business hours. You need to have the support that your business needs or can afford to justify.

Service availability and reliability

This should say how much of the time the service is supposed to be delivered and whether they guarantee that it will or accept some penalty or price reduction. It is often specified in terms of percentages such as 99% of a given time period. Again you must understand what this means for you: 99% over a month in 'normal' working hours means that per month there will be no more than roughly two hours when the service is not present.

Related to this is the maximum length and number of service breaks that can occur. For example you might meet 99% availability (normal hours) over a year with a maximum break (if all at once) of 20 hours, which would be nearly three working days. You might want to restrict the maximum period of non-availability to say half a day. All of this affects cost.

Customer support

This should contain all of the contact details for obtaining the service (e.g. helpdesk phone numbers); it might also include websites and other DIY sources of help.

Service performance, tracking and reporting

This is related to availability and has similar points to consider (e.g. cost that you can justify for the service you need). This may include terms such as MTTF (mean time to fix), FTF (first time fixes as a percentage of all calls), ATTA (average time to answer: the average time, usually in seconds, that it takes for a call to be answered by the service desk) and TSF (time service factor: the percentage of calls answered within a definite time frame, e.g. 80% in 20 seconds). This may include time for batch processes such as payroll runs etc. It also includes how the service will be reported (e.g. monthly reports, live statistics on a webpage, meetings and so forth).

Continuity and security

This covers how the supplier will support continuity of service (e.g. in the event of 'disasters') and will include such things as offsite backups, standby equipment and the like. Security will cover both physical security issues and things such as password control, what happens in the case of unauthorised access, viruses and related issues.

Service reviews

This should describe how, when, where and by whom the delivered service will be reviewed. Typically there may be monthly, quarterly and annual reviews with different objectives in terms of tactical and strategic goals for service improvement.

Problem management

This is a description of escalation and related processes for dealing with problems that are not resolved first time, within the normal processes. For example this will cover unusual technical problems that need a fix from the original authors of the software (e.g. Microsoft in the case of Windows).

Change management

This is how any changes will be considered and implemented and what the process is. Note that some agreements include charges for evaluating change requests: be careful of this. Others will allow a specific number within the year and so forth.

Legal compliance and resolution of disputes*

These are contractual terms that set out how serious disputes that are not resolved through normal processes are dealt with, for example in the case of no default by the supplier, non-payment by the client and so forth.

Customer duties and responsibilities*

What you have to do in order for the supplier to deliver the service will be described here.

IPR and confidential Information*

The most likely issues here will be escrow (see also the section below on terms to watch out for) and protection of your intellectual property rights (IPR). You need to be happy that you have control over the IPR and confidentiality of any business critical data. Consider also the Data Protection Act here (a subject in its own right; see the reference list).

Termination*

This may be in the general T&Cs or specifically described here. It will cover what the grounds are for termination and what happens after termination takes place (e.g. handover, continuity etc.).

> **NOTE**
>
> Items marked with an asterisk above are often part of the main contract not the SLA; in an SME environment it is likely that the two may be merged so they are mentioned here to be on the safe side.

GENERAL TERMS AND CONDITIONS

This section is intended to provide a primer for those looking at the contractual side of the agreements they sign up to. It is not intended to replace the use of a suitably qualified legal adviser, but is intended to give you some idea what they are talking about. It is probably true to say that the only trade more accustomed to jargon than IT is the legal profession. In an ideal world they would explain everything to you in plain English so that you knew what it meant; sadly this is not always the case. In fact a quick look at the T&Cs that come with the majority of software products will show anything but the plain and understandable. Hopefully some clues will be found in this section: in particular the section on terms to watch out for covers the general structure and contents of a typical UK contract.

Performance and capacity

For hardware performance manufacturers specifications will cover items such as disk capacity, memory, CPU speed and so forth. There may be specifications covering items such as the number of transactions the system can support in a given time. However, these and more general service delivery measures are usually covered in the form of an SLA for services (see the earlier section on SLAs). Where performance is a specific issue you will need to agree on how it is to be measured: this may involve specialist activities such as benchmarking.

Payment terms and variations

It is important to understand all of the ins and outs of how you pay for the service or goods that you have agreed to buy. Unless you are simply buying equipment the price is likely to have both fixed and variable elements, some of which may be conditional on specific triggers. For instance user licences may be 'banded' in that up to 10 users will cost £X per user per year, but 11 to 25 may cost a lower figure of £Y per user per year.

There can be quite complex sets of conditions in how payment variations are triggered. What is vital is that you have a complete understanding of what these are and what they mean for you and your business. Flexibility can be more important than absolute price.

Sale of Goods Act

Under the Sale of Goods Act 1979 traders must sell goods that are as described and of satisfactory quality. This applies to all goods sold. What this means is that if they sell you an eight-port router, it should have eight ports and they should all work as described. If it has eight ports, but you can only use say six of them at a time, then you can return it and get your money back. If it says it comes in grey, then you do not have to accept it if it is blue and so forth.

Supply of Goods and Services Act

The concepts of the Sale of Goods Act 1979 were further extended by the Supply of Goods and Services Act 1982. The DTI website (see the list of useful websites at the end of the book) describes the act as follows:

> The Supply of Goods and Services Act 1982 requires traders to provide services to a proper standard of workmanship. Furthermore, if a definite completion date or a price has not been fixed then the work must be completed within a reasonable time and for a reasonable charge.
>
> Also, any material used or goods supplied in providing the service must be of satisfactory quality.
>
> The law treats failure to meet these obligations as breach of contract and consumers would be entitled to seek redress, if necessary through the civil courts.

Terms to watch out for

Contractual 'nasties' and 'gotchas' can be spotted by a lawyer reviewing the terms for you. However, major points to look for when you initially look through the terms are given in the following sections. As stated before this is not a substitute for professional advice, but can help you to understand what they are talking about.

Assignment

The client or customer should be able to assign its software licences to a third party so that fresh licences do not have to be purchased by that third party if it purchases the customer's organisation. Some suppliers do not allow this to happen and it can be a hidden cost that is only discovered during a due diligence process in a takeover.

Standard or boilerplate

Some 'standard' legal clauses crop up as part of a contract, usually at the end. Your legal adviser will tell you if there is anything to worry about.

Entire agreement clauses

This is a bit of a get-out clause. Often during negotiations suppliers make various promises. By having an 'entire agreement' clause the suppliers limit their liability to what is in the agreement: you cannot enforce anything that you thought you were promised before, although this does not exclude cases where they act fraudulently.

For this reason you may wish to include a statement in any ITT/ITN document you produce to the effect that their proposals are considered to be part of any subsequent contract.

Escrow

As the source code for applications and software is not normally provided you are at risk if anything happens to the supplier. Ensure that a copy is deposited with a third-party agent, for example with a bank. Then if the supplier goes out of business you will be able to access the source code from the third party and get someone to maintain it. This can be a tricky area, but a realistic compromise can usually be achieved.

Exit clauses and conditions

All contracts need to cover things such as what happens when there are significant breaches of contract conditions (i.e. non-delivery of service, non-payment by client etc.), bankruptcy and so on. However, because business is always changing you may also want to think about things such as having break points after certain periods, perhaps every year.

You may also want termination for convenience, for example upon a notice period of 90 days. You may wish to have this in place in case your supplier is taken over and you do not get on with the new owners. You may also want to consider having the option to keep a core service whilst dropping specific elements, for example if you wanted to stop using and supporting a particular software product.

Exit plan

This is related to the clauses that can cause an exit. There needs to be a plan in place that says what happens and in what sequence so that you are not left high and dry with no means of keeping your business going. This is relevant to bespoke and 'enterprise' solutions rather than, for example, word processing packages.

Force majeure

This makes sure that you or the supplier is not responsible for failing to perform contractual obligations due to events beyond reasonable control. For instance a supplier may be unable to deliver equipment because the road is flooded. Some examples are not this simple and open to debate, for example staff being off sick. Ask your legal adviser for help if you have anything further you wish to define like this.

Intellectual property

You need to be sure that you own or have rights to any intellectual property that you use as a result of the contract. If you do not then you are taking a risk that someone else may have the right to stop you using the software that your business depends on. You also need to cover what might happen if the supplier ceases to trade or is taken over.

Law

This matters: if you are an English or Welsh company then it should say the terms should be governed by English and Welsh law. It should also state the jurisdiction where the case is to be heard, again England and Wales.

Limit of liability

This is vital. You want to be indemnified not just against any faults or non-availability of the software or services you get from the supplier but also for any consequential losses from such failures. For example if your billing systems fails for a week and you cannot trade then you want more than just your money back: you also want compensation for loss of business. You need to negotiate appropriate limits. It is worth noting that with many major suppliers of, for example, office software that they limit their liability to almost nothing: this is take it or leave it. However, with bespoke software, systems or 'enterprise' applications you should have a reasonable agreement in place that protects you.

Price

You will have a price agreed and general terms in place. In addition you should look at payment terms such as 30 days (or longer) in arrears as this gives you a lever if you feel the supplier has failed to deliver.

Ideally also get them to agree that they will not charge you more than any other customer they service: this protects you from them giving better deals to bigger clients.

Where prices are reviewed annually (or any other period) try and get an agreement that puts a limit (e.g. an index such as the retail price index or an appropriate trade index) on how much the increases can be.

Software

This is important. You need to know not only what software you are getting (off-the-shelf and bespoke components) but also what support is included. For example will this include any modifications, enhancements, new releases and new versions? If not, then there can be cost implications in the future. This applies to documentation as well.

You should check that there is no outstanding litigation relating to the software and ask that they certify it to be virus and bug free (as far as they can).

You should also make sure that the supplier has the right to use any software components they supply you with and that this right cannot be taken away in the time you need to use the systems.

Support and maintenance

The best way to do this is to have a SLA (see the section on SLAs earlier in this chapter) that covers the services (including those related to software) to be supplied together with the levels to be achieved and credits or penalties for not meeting them. A key point is to make sure you are happy with the support before you agree to the use of particular software (see the earlier section on licences). You need to be happy with both of these: good support with onerous licence conditions (or vice versa) can be bad news.

Third-party rights

This is effectively a means of limiting liability. Contracts will often say that third parties have no rights to enforce the terms of the contract. The benefits of the contract do not pass down the line. Your customers cannot enforce the terms on your suppliers or yourself.

Waiver

The waiver clause typically states that if a party decides to waive its rights to claim against the other party for a breach of the terms, then it can do so later on if it needs to. In other words you can change your mind later.

Severability

What this normally says is that if some part of the contract proves to be invalid or unenforceable you can strip it out of the contract and the rest will still stand.

DUE DILIGENCE

This is a phrase that comes up whenever there is any take over of activities, for example when outsourcing. It has its source in corporate takeovers and our non-QAed source Wikipedia.org gives the following definition:

> Due diligence is a term used for a number of concepts involving either the performance of an investigation of a business or person, or the performance of an act with a certain standard of care. It can be a legal obligation, but the term will more commonly apply to voluntary investigations.

The following was given as an example: 'The process through which a potential acquirer evaluates a target company or its assets for acquisition.' In terms of an SME procurement this comes down to the supplier potentially having a duty of care to ask you questions prior to finalising a contract and the client being required to answer them. If this affects you then you definitely need professional advice.

ENVIRONMENTAL ISSUES

There is a growing volume of environmental legislation that applies across all areas of an SME's business. With particular relevance to IT procurement is the subsequent disposal of the hardware (and also any packaging that came with it; this may apply to software to as it will include paper and plastic and possibly metal, such as CDs and DVDs).

The Waste Electrical and Electronic Equipment (WEEE) Directive 2002/96/EC and 2003/108/EC (WEEE Directive) came into force in the UK on 1 January 2007 with full producer responsibility beginning in July 2007. Under this producers became responsible for financing the collection, treatment, recycling and recovery of WEEE ('producer responsibility'). This does not just apply to new products. Producers became responsible collectively for goods already on the market.

The legislation became European law on 13 February 2003 and European member states had to implement it by 13 August 2004. Retailers had to establish in-store take back or alternative collection systems by 13 August 2005.

Targets for recycling and recovery of materials and components from the separately collected WEEE had to be met by 31 December 2006. The directive came into full force on 1 January 2007 and full producer responsibility began on 7 July 2007.

From the point of view of your procurement you should be aware that your supplier will have to take the goods back for disposal from you, at no extra charge, for proper recycling or disposal. This does not mean they have to collect it from you, so you need to consider this as part of your costs for a new procurement.

SUMMARY

For simple hardware and consumables purchases, the legal issues in the UK are no worse than for any other purchase an SME is likely to make. *Caveat emptor* (let the buyer beware) as usual but at this level IT is just another consumer purchase: watch out for the extended warranty they may push at you but by and large there is nothing to worry about.

However software and bespoke procurements are a different issue. Even buying ordinary office productivity software such as word processing and spreadsheets can bring up licensing issues. Once you start buying IT services, be it from an ISP, a helpdesk or support for bespoke developments with specific service levels then legal matters become rather more significant. Unless your organisation includes its own legal experts, then for anything non-standard the best advice is to get help from a suitably qualified and experienced professional.

References and Further Reading

> **NOTE**
>
> Not all of these books and publications are currently in print; you may need to obtain them from dealers in second-hand bookshops or from a library.

> **NOTE**
>
> The *For Dummies* series covers most popular applications and technologies (e.g. MS office, PCs, Macs and so forth) published by Wiley, New York.

Blackstaff, M. (2006) *Finance for IT Decision Makers: A Practical Handbook for Buyers, Sellers and Managers* (2nd edition). British Computer Society, Swindon. ISBN-10: 1902505735; ISBN-13: 978-1902505732.

BSI (2007) The WEEE Directive. www.bsi-global.com/en/Standards-and-Publications/Industry-Sectors/Manufacturing/WEEE-directive/

Burns, P. (2006) *The Beginner's Guide to Broadband and Wireless Internet*. Summersdale, Chichester. ISBN-10: 1840244992; ISBN-13: 978-1840244991.

Churchouse, C. and Churchouse, J. (1999) *Managing Projects*. Gower, Aldershot. ISBN-10: 0566080982; ISBN-13: 978-0566080982.

Cory, T. (2003) *Brainstorming: Techniques for New Ideas*. iUniverse.com, Lincoln, NE. ISBN-10: 0595751407; ISBN-13: 978-0595751402

Davis, H. (2004) *Absolute Beginner's Guide to Wi-Fi Wireless Networking*. Que Corporation, Carmel, IN. ISBN-10: 0789731150; ISBN-13: 978-0789731159.

DTI Small Business Service (2006) SME Statistics for 2005. http://stats.berr.gov.uk/ed/sme/smestats2005-ukspr.pdf

Holden, S. and Francis, M. (2004) *The Beginner's Guide to Computers and the Internet: Windows XP Edition*. Summersdale, Chichester. ISBN-10: 1840243961; ISBN-13: 978-1840243963.

Kennedy, G. (1997) *Everything is Negotiable.* Random House, London. ISBN-10: 0099243822.

McManus, J. (2003) *Risk Management in Software Development Projects.* Butterworth-Heinemann, London. ISBN-10: 0750658673; ISBN-13: 978-0750658676.

McManus, J. (2004) *Computer Weekly,* 20 July.

Nickson, D. (2003) *The Bid Manager's Handbook.* Gower, Aldershot. ISBN-10: 0566085127; ISBN-13: 978-0566085123.

Nickson, D. and Siddons, S. (1996) *Business Communications (Made Simple).* Butterworth-Heinemann, London. ISBN-10: 0750625724; ISBN-13: 978-0750625722.

Nickson, D. and Siddons, S. (1997) *Managing Projects.* Butterworth-Heinemann, London. ISBN-10: 0750634715; ISBN-13: 978-0750634717.

Nickson, D. and Siddons, S. (2005) *Business Communications 101.* Lulu.com, Morrisville, NC. ISBN-10: 1411691083; ISBN-13: 978-1411691087.

Nickson, D. and Siddons, S. (2006) *Project Management Disasters: And How to Survive Them.* Kogan Page, London. ISBN-10: 074944780X; ISBN-13: 978-0749447809.

Op de Coul, J. C. (2005) *IT Services Procurement Based on ISPL – A Pocket Guide,* Van Bon, J. (ed.). Van Haren Publishing, Zaltbommel. ISBN-10: 9077212507; ISBN-13: 978-9077212509.

PCG (2007) Budget Report. www.pcg.org.uk/cms/index.php?option= com_content&task=view&id=2257&Itemid=1

Pegge, S. (2006) Small Business Survey in 2006. Lloyds TSB Business.

Rich, J. R. (2003) *Brain Storm: Tap into Your Creativity to Generate Awesome Ideas and Remarkable Results.* Career Press, Franklin Lakes, NJ. ISBN-10: 1564146685; ISBN-13: 978-1564146687.

Stationery Office Books (2005) Introduction to ITIL. The Stationery Office, London. ISBN-10: 0113309732; ISBN-13: 978-0113309733.

Van Bon, J. (ed.) (2005) *Foundations of IT Service Management: Based on ITIL* (2nd revised edition). Van Haren Publishing, Zaltbommel. ISBN-10: 9077212582; ISBN-13: 978-9077212585.

Useful Websites

> **NOTE**
>
> These links were valid at the time of writing. However, such links are notorious for changing/disappearing at short notice. If the link no longer seems to work it is suggested you try is as a starting point in a search engine or visit the home page of the relevant site.

Professional institutes

www.bcs.org/
www.pmi.org/
www.apm.org.uk/
www.cipd.co.uk/default.cipd
www.supplymanagement.co.uk/
www.cips.org/

SaaS

www.google.com/a/
www.sun.com/software/star/openoffice/
www.starbase.co.uk/enterprise_applications_citrix.asp

QA and standards

http://en.wikipedia.org/wiki/Quality_assurance
www.ogc.gov.uk/documentation_and_templates_project_quality_plan.asp
www.best-management-practice.com/IT-Service-Management-ITIL/
http://projekte.fast.de/ISPL/
www.bsi-global.com/en/Standards-and-Publications/Industry-Sectors/Manufacturing/WEEE-directive/
www.bsi-global.com/en/Standards-and-Publications/How-we-can-help-you/Business/Small-Businesses/
www.bsonline.bsi-global.com/server/index.jsp
www.bsi-global.com/
www.standardsuk.com/

Industry organisations

www.fast.org.uk/

Government

http://online.ogcbuyingsolutions.gov.uk/news/
www.ogc.gov.uk/
www.berr.gov.uk/ (was DTI)

Legal

http://en.wikipedia.org/wiki/Due_diligence
www.lawsociety.org.uk/home.law
www.dti.gov.uk/consumers/buying-selling/ucp/index.html
www.dti.gov.uk/consumers/buying-selling/sale-supply/sale-of-good-act/page8600.html
www.dti.gov.uk/consumers/buying-selling/sale-supply/supply-of-goods-services/page8628.html

Miscellaneous

www.pcg.org.uk/cms/index.php?option=com_content&task=view&id=2257&Itemid=1

Organisations List

Association for Project Management, 150 West Wycombe Road, High Wycombe, Buckinghamshire HP12 3AE, UK

The British Computer Society (BCS), First Floor, Block D, North Star House, North Star Avenue, Swindon SN2 1FA, UK

BSI British Standards, 389 Chiswick High Road, London W4 4AL, UK

Chartered Institute of Personnel and Development (CIPD), 151 The Broadway, London SW19 1JQ, UK

Chartered Institute of Purchasing and Supply (CIPS), Easton House, Easton on the Hill, Stamford, Lincolnshire PE9 3NZ, UK

Federation Against Software Theft (FAST) Limited (by guarantee), York House, 18 York Road, Maidenhead SL6 1SF, UK

Microsoft, Microsoft Campus, Thames Valley Park, Reading, Berkshire RG6 1WG, UK

Office of Government Commerce (OGC), Rosebery Court, St Andrew's Business Park, Norwich, Norfolk NR7 0HS, UK

Project Management Institute (PMI), Four Campus Boulevard, Newtown Square, PA 19073-3299, USA

Sun Microsystems, Regis House, 45 King William Street, London EC4R 9AN, UK

Index

Other products and services from the British Computer Society, which might be of interest to you include:

Publishing

BCS publications, including books, magazine and peer-review journals, provide readers with informed content on business, management, legal, and emerging technological issues, supporting the professional, academic and practical needs of the IT community. Subjects covered include Business Process Management, IT law for managers and transition management. **www.bcs.org/publications**

BCS Professional Products and Services

BCS Membership. By joining BCS you will become a part of the UK's industry body for IT professionals, and the leading Chartered Engineering Institution for IT. Our aim is to be directly relevant to the priorities, needs and aspirations of our individual members at every stage of their career. **www.bcs.org/join**

BCS Group Membership Scheme. BCS offers a group membership scheme to organizations who wish to sign up their IT workforce as professional members (MBCS). By encouraging their IT professionals to join BCS through our group scheme organizations are ensuring that they create a path to Chartered Status with the post nominals CITP (Chartered IT Professional). www.bcs.org.uk/forms/group

BCS promotes the use of the **SFIAplus™** IT skills, training & development standard in a range of professional development products and services for employers leading to accreditation. These include **BCS IT Job Describer, BCS Skills Manager** and **BCS Career Developer**. www.bcs.org/products

Qualifications

Information Systems Examination Board (ISEB) qualifications are the industry standard both here and abroad, and with over 100,000 practitioners now qualified, it is proof of their popularity. They ensure that IT professionals develop the skills, knowledge and confidence to perform to their full potential. There is a huge range on offer covering all major areas of IT. In essence, ISEB qualifications are for forward looking individuals and companies who want to stay ahead – who are serious about driving business forward. **www.iseb.org.uk**

BCS Professional Examinations are internationally recognised and essential qualifications for a career in computing and information technology (IT). At their highest level, the examinations are examined to the academic level of a UK university honours degree and acknowledge practical experience and academic ability. **www.bcs.org/exams**

European Computer Driving Licence™ (ECDL) is the internationally recognised computer skills qualification which enables people to demonstrate their competence on computer skills. ECDL is managed in the UK by the BCS. ECDL Advanced has been introduced to take computer skills certification to the next level and teaches extensive knowledge of particular computing tools. **www.ecdl.co.uk**

Networking and Events

BCS's Specialist Groups and Branches provide excellent professional networking opportunities by keeping members abreast of latest developments, discussing topical issues and making useful contacts. **www.bcs.org**

The Society's programme of social events, lectures, awards schemes, and competitions provides more opportunities to network. **www.bcs.org/events**

Further Information

This information was correct at the time of publication, but could change in the future. For the latest information, please contact:
The British Computer Society
First Floor, Block D
North Star House
North Star Avenue
Swindon
SN2 1FA, UK.
Telephone: 0845 300 4417 (UK only) or + 44 1793 417 424 (overseas)
E-mail: bcshq@hq.bcs.org.uk
Web: www.bcs.org

Jude Umeh

The World Beyond Digital Rights Management

Jude Umeh

Digital content owners and commercial stakeholders face a constant battle to protect their intellectual property and commercial rights. Jude Umeh outlines the issues behind this battle, current solutions to the problem and looks to the future beyond digital rights management.

ISBN: 978-1-902505-87-9
Price: £34.95 Size: 246 x 172mm Paperback: 320pp
Published: Oct 2007 www.bcs.org/books/drm

IT Law An ISEB Foundation

Jon Fell (Editor)

IT professionals not only need to know the technology, they should be aware of how the law applies to the technology. This is a guide to the main aspects of law that an IT professional is most likely to come up against. A textbook for the 'ISEB Foundation Certificate in IT Law.'

ISBN: 978-1-902505-80-0
Price: £24.95 Size: 246 x 172mm Paperback: 320pp
Published: Oct 2007 www.bcs.org/books/isebITLaw

Jon Fell (Editor),
John Antell, Jonathan Exell,
Stephen Mason, Vivian Picton,
Adrian Roberts-Walsh, Louise Townsend

A Manager's Guide to IT Law

Jeremy Newton and Jeremy Holt (Editors)

This comprehensive guide to IT-related legal issues explains, in plain English, the most relevant legal frameworks, with examples from actual case law used to illustrate the most common problems. Including: IT contracts; systems procurement contracts; employment problems; instructing an IT consultant; intellectual property law; escrow; outsourcing; data protection.

ISBN: 978-1-902505-55-8
Price: £29.95 Size: 246 x 172mm Paperback: 180pp
Published: July 2004 www.bcs.org/books/itlaw

Data Protection & Compliance in Context
Stewart Room

This pragmatic guide provides practical advice on protecting data privacy under the Data Protection Act, human rights laws and freedom of information legislation; and gives a platform for building compliance strategies. Stewart Room, is the chair of the National Association of Data Protection and Freedom of Information Officers (NADPO).

ISBN: 978-1-902505-78-7
Price: £34.95 Size: 246 x 172mm Paperback: 304pp
Published: Oct 2006 www.bcs.org/books/dataprotection

Principles of Data Management
Facilitating Information Sharing
Keith Gordon

A practical guide to managing data – an increasingly valuble corporate asset in all organisations. Information is a key resource as important as equipment, assets, estate and capital. Invaluable for managing, marketing and IT directors and all business managers.

ISBN: 978-1-902505-84-8
Price: £29.95 Size 246 x 172 Paperback: 274pp
Published: Aug 2007 www.bcs.org/books/datamanagement

Practical Data Migration
John Morris

This guide contains techniques and strategies for ensuring data migration projects achieve maximum return on investment; ideas on rescuing ailing projects; and a model of best practice to be used for implementation of the methods. All blended with real life examples and clear definitions of commonly used jargon.

ISBN: 978-1-902505-71-8
Price: £29.95 Size: 246 x 172mm Paperback: 224pp
Published: May 2006 www.bcs.org/books/datamigration

World Class IT Service Delivery

Peter Wheatcroft

A manual on reaching and sustaining best practice in terms of performance, delivery and outlook in IT services to avoid customer dissatisfaction. Essential for IT service managers, IT directors, managers and procurement specialists.

ISBN: 978-1-902505-82-4
Price: £29.95 Size: 246 x 172 Paperback: 192pp
Published: May 2007 www.bcs.org/books/servicedelivery

Global Services
Moving to a Level Playing Field
Mark Kobayashi-Hillary and Dr Richard Sykes

Global Sourcing experts give an overview of how globalisation of the service industry is changing businesses and opening new opportunities to industries. A guide for managing, finance and IT directors and purchasing managers in all industries.

ISBN: 978-1-902505-83-1
Price: £29.95 Size: 246 x 172 Paperback: 192pp
Published: Apr 2007 www.bcs.org/books/globalservices

A Guide to Global Sourcing
Offshore outsourcing and other global delivery models
Elizabeth Anne Sparrow

The opportunities and obstacles associated with offshore outsourcing and other global delivery models. Country-by-country analysis of offshore services available.

ISBN: 978-1-902505-61-9
Price: £34.95 Size: 246 x 172mm Paperback: 196pp
Published: Nov 2004 www.bcs.org/books/globalsourcing

A Pragmatic Guide to
Business Process Modelling
Jon Holt

Explores all aspects of process modelling from process analysis to process documentation by applying a standard modelling notation, UML. Guidance for directors and managers on business process modelling to improve processes, productivity and profitability.

ISBN: 978-1-902505-66-4
Price: £29.95 Size: 246 x 172mm Paperback: 184pp
Published: Sept 2005 www.bcs.org/books/processmodelling

Business Process Management
A Rigorous Approach
Martyn A. Ould

A rigorous way of understanding the mass of concurrent, collaborative activity that goes on within an organisation, giving a solid basis for developing IT systems that actually support a business' processes and improving efficiency and profitability.

ISBN: 978-1-902505-60-2
Price: £34.95 Size: 246 x 172mm Paperback: 364pp
Published: Jan 2005 www.bcs.org/books/bpm

Business Analysis
Debra Paul and Donald Yeates (Editors)

A practical introductory guide for improving the effectiveness of IT and its alignment with an organisation's business objectives. Covers strategy analysis, modelling business systems/processes, business case development, managing change, requirements engineering and information resource management.

ISBN: 978-1-902505-70-1
Price: £29.95 Size: 246 x 172mm Paperback: 256pp
Published: Apr 2006 www.bcs.org/books/businessanalysis

Finance for IT Decision Makers
A practical handbook for buyers, sellers and managers (2nd Edition)

Michael Blackstaff

This covers aspects of finance relevant to professionals who make or influence decisions about IT. Written in plain language with practical examples, it explains: how to construct a financial case for IT projects; financing methods; current standards and legislation; cost/benefit analysis; investment evaluation methods; budgeting, costing and pricing; and more.

ISBN: 978-1-902505-73-2

Price: £34.95 Size: 246 x 172mm Paperback: 324pp
Published: July 2006 www.bcs.org/books/finance

Project Management in The Real World
Shortcuts to success

Elizabeth Harrin

This book provides a short cut to project management experience; it summarizes over 250 years of expertise from experienced project managers. It offers hints and tips on all aspects of project management including: managing project budgets; managing project scope; managing project teams; managing project plans; and managing yourself.

ISBN: 978-1-902505-81-7

Price: £24.95 Size: 246 x 172mm Paperback: 225pp
Published: Nov 2006 www.bcs.org/books/realworldPM

Project Management for IT-Related Projects
Textbook for the ISEB Foundation Certificate in IS Project Management

Bob Hughes (Editor)

The principles of IT-related project management, including project planning, monitoring and control, change management, risk management and communication between project stakeholders. Encompasses the entire syllabus of the 'ISEB Foundation Certificate in IS Project Management'.

ISBN: 978-1-902505-58-9

Price: £24.95 Size: 297 x 210mm Paperback: 148pp
Published: Aug 2004 www.bcs.org/books/projectmanagement

Software Testing An ISEB Foundation

Brian Hambling (Editor)

Providing a practical insight into the world of software testing, this book explains the basic steps of the testing process and how to perform effective tests. It supports the revised 'ISEB Foundation Certificate in Software Testing' and includes self-assessment exercises, worked examples and sample exam questions.

ISBN: 978-1-902505-79-4
Price: £24.95 Size: 246 x 172mm Paperback: 220pp
Published: Sept 2006 www.bcs.org/books/softwaretesting

Professional Issues in Information Technology

Frank Bott

This book explores the relationship between technological change, society and the law, and the powerful role that computers and computer professionals play in a technological society. Designed to accompany the BCS Professional Examination core Diploma module: 'Professional Issues in Information Systems Practice'.

ISBN: 978-1-902505-65-7
Price: £24.95 Size: 246 x 172mm Paperback: 248pp
Published: May 2005 www.bcs.org/books/professionalissues

Invisible Architecture
The benefits of aligning people, processes and technology

Jenny Ure & Gudrun Jaegersberg

The biggest problems faced in implementing computer systems, especially across different countries, are often not technical – they are 'socio-technical'. *Invisible Architecture* uses real examples to highlight the potential for harnessing 'soft' factors to competitive advantage.

ISBN: 978-1-902505-59-6
Price: £34.95 Size: 246 x 172mm Paperback: 104pp
Published: Mar 2005 www.bcs.org/books/invisiblearchitecture

BCS ORDER FORM

To order your book(s), please complete this form and send it to:
BCS Books, Turpin Distribution, Pegasus Drive, Stratton Business Park,
Biggleswade, Bedfordshire, SG18 8TQ, UK.
Fax: +44 (0)1767 601640 Tel: +44 (0)1767 604951
Enquiries to: Custserv@turpin-distribution.com
BCS Books are also available in all good bookshops.

	Price	Qty	BCS Member Price	Qty
The World Beyond Digital Rights Management	£34.95		£30	
IT Law: An ISEB Foundation	£24.95		£20	
A Manager's Guide to IT Law	£29.95		£20	
Data Protection and Compliance in Context	£34.95		£30	
Principles of Data Management	£29.95		£25	
Practical Data Migration	£29.95		£25	
World Class IT Service Delivery	£29.95		£20	
Global Services: Moving to a Level Playing Field	£29.95		£20	
A Guide To Global Sourcing	£34.95		£20	
A Pragmatic Guide to Business Process Modelling	£29.95		£25	
Business Process Management	£34.95		£30	
Business Analysis	£29.95		£20	
Finance for IT Decision Makers	£34.95		£25	
Project Management in the Real World	£24.95		£15	
Project Management for IT-Related Projects	£24.95		£15	
Software Testing	£24.95		£15	
Professional Issues in Information Technology	£24.95		£15	
Invisible Architecture	£34.95		£20	

P&P: UK £2.75 for the first book, plus 75p for any additional items.
Europe £5. Rest of world £12.

Postage: £ ____

Total: £ ____

Title: .... Initials: .... Surname: ....

Address: ....

BCS membership number (if applicable): ....

Telephone: .... Email: ....

I enclose a cheque ☐ made payable to 'The British Computer Society' or please charge my:

☐ Visa ☐ Mastercard ☐ Switch/Maestro ☐ American Express (please indicate)

Start date (Maestro/Switch only): .... Issue number (Maestro/Switch only): ....

Expiry date: .... Card number: ....

Name as it appears on card: ....

Signature: ....

*BooksUpdate service: please mark this box to receive occasional emails about new titles and
special offers on BCS publications (you can opt out from receiving these communications at any time).* ☐